125

TWELVE TWENTY-FIVE

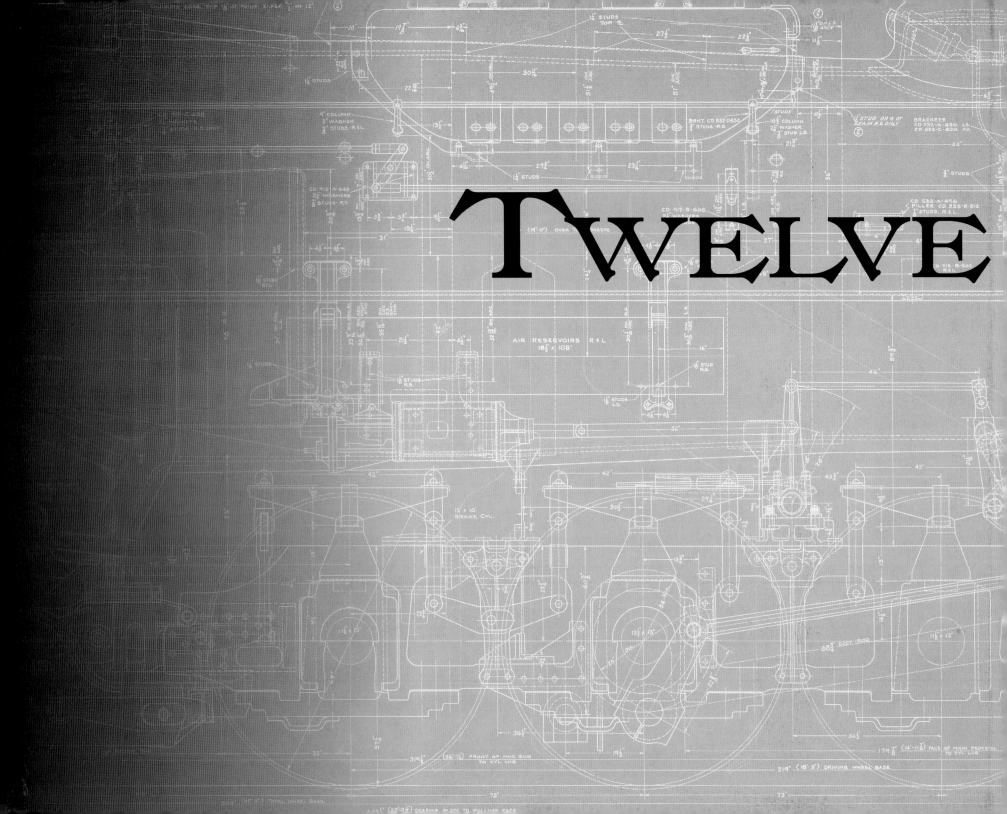

Twelve

TWENTY-FIVE

THE LIFE AND TIMES OF A STEAM LOCOMOTIVE

Kevin P. Keefe

MICHIGAN STATE UNIVERSITY PRESS | *East Lansing*

♾ The paper used in this publication meets the minimum requirements
of ANSI/NISO Z39.48-1992 (R 1997) (Permanence of Paper).

MICHIGAN STATE UNIVERSITY PRESS
East Lansing, Michigan 48823-5245

Printed and bound in China.

22 21 20 19 18 17 16   1 2 3 4 5 6 7 8 9 10

LIBRARY OF CONGRESS CATALOGING-IN-PUBLICATION DATA
Keefe, Kevin P., author.
Twelve twenty-five : the life and times of a steam locomotive / Kevin P. Keefe.
pages cm
Includes bibliographical references and index.
ISBN 978-1-61186-202-7 (cloth : alk. paper)—ISBN 978-1-61186-203-4 (pbk. : alk. paper)—ISBN
978-1-60917-488-0 (pdf) 1. Pere Marquette 1225 (Steam locomotive)—History. 2. Pere Marquette
Railway—History. 3. Steam locomotives—Michigan—History. I. Title.
TJ603.3.P48K44 2016
625.26'1—dc23
2015029318

Book design by Charlie Sharp, Sharp Des!gns, Lansing, Michigan
Cover design by Erin Kirk New
ENDPAPERS: Pere Marquette locomotive No. 1225, detail from the side elevation drawing.
Lima Locomotive Works Collection, California State Railroad Museum Library.
COVER: Pere Marquette 1225 © Jeff Mast Photography, used courtesy of the photographer.
All rights reserved.

Michigan State University Press is a member of the Green Press Initiative and is
committed to developing and encouraging ecologically responsible publishing
practices. For more information about the Green Press Initiative and the use of
recycled paper in book publishing, please visit *www.greenpressinitiative.org.*

Visit Michigan State University Press at *www.msupress.org*

To the girl in McDonel Hall

◆

Contents

FOREWORD

William L. Withuhn

The "Christmas Engine"—the same locomotive, reproduced in animation, made famous in *The Polar Express* starring Tom Hanks—that's 1225.

It beats me why the film, a perennial holiday treasure, doesn't show the engine's number clearly. As far as I know, no other active steam locomotive is numbered for Christmas. It's no fluke or nostalgic reference: Pere Marquette No. 1225 came out of the Lima Locomotive Works in Ohio in 1941 to speed the nation's colossally accelerating production to support the defense of Western democracy.

The 1225 embodies another kind of treasure—it's one of the last great engines from the 125-year history of steam power on the nation's railroads. Our freight railroads, now prospering but far less costly for shippers than ever before, all run on the superb transportation system that steam built. Yes, a third of U.S. track mileage that once interconnected the country is gone, but the remaining miles, nearly all rebuilt and surrounded by new associated facilities, carry more rail freight traffic than ever. Today's railroads haul nearly two-and-a-half times more than at the peak of World War II.

Not only is 1225 big and brawny, it's handsome. My wife, Gail (granddaughter of a railroad stationmaster), asks: "How can something so huge and industrial be 'handsome'?" I guess it's in the eye of the beholder. I look at 1225 and say, "That's one of the finest-looking big steamers ever"—great proportions, external systems and piping blending nicely with the engine's lines, wheels arranged gracefully, classic cab, no awkwardness anywhere. Despite its massive weight, it looks light on its feet. It could indeed run fast, 70 miles per hour with a big train for hours on end.

I rode in the cab of a sister engine once—more than an hour at night in the cab of an identical 2-8-4, with a veteran crew that had run the engine in active service in the 1950s. I was amazed. Immediately at the change of a signal, the engineer sounded the bell and two whistle calls. In seconds, the heavy train rolled without a shudder or slip. In two driver revolutions the train was at 20 miles per hour and accelerating rapidly toward full road speed.

The stack bark was incredible. On the other side of the cab, the fireman sat at full attention (he was portly and short; his feet didn't even reach the floor). His control of the fire was acute: small changes only to the stoker speed, and he frequently noted the engine's throttle position. Every change in throttle brought a bit more or less stoker speed. The boiler-pressure needle could have been glued in place, holding perhaps three pounds below safety-valve opening. He glanced often at the holes in the firedoor. Those little holes shined brightly, like intensely white carbon-arc spotlights. He had such sharp control that he rose only twice in an hour to inspect the fire. He didn't use the scoop; no reason to, I supposed. Mostly, the rock-steady pressure and the brightness of all the firedoor holes told the tale.

Professionalism revealed itself. Few words were exchanged, just the calling of signals to each other. Both crew watched intensely ahead. Back then, I'd never before been in a main-line cab at speed, and I was surprised by the short distance the locomotive's big headlight seemed to penetrate the enveloping dark. The fireman often raised his right thumb up briefly on left-hand curves while he focused ahead, letting the engineer—who couldn't see around left curves—know that eyeballs were on duty, protecting the train. I discovered that a skilled fireman is truly the copilot of a steam-hauled train, a lesson I never forgot. Of course, both members of the engine crew knew precisely where each signal, curve, speed restriction, grade change, switch, road crossing (private or public), culvert, and bridge was located, milepost by exact milepost.

Both the engine I rode and 1225 share a great heritage. Will Woodard, the remarkable chief designer for the upstart Lima Locomotive Works, created the 2-8-4 type. Woodard was a lover of classical music and fine cigars, gardener of prize roses, and owner of a gorgeous 47-foot Herreshoff motor yacht named *Ariel II* on which he welcomed guests. He was also the husband of Phoebe, who insisted when Lima hired her husband away from the American Locomotive Company that she *would not* move "out West" from New York, where they lived. So Lima paid for a working office with a senior draftsman in New York City, and most weeks Woodard commuted via the Pennsylvania Railroad to Lima for about three days on-site. Will and son George were fond companions. George helped design America's first jet fighter, the P-59A of 1942. Earlier, his father said, "If I can get ten more years out of the steam locomotive, I'll be happy." He succeeded.

The 2-8-4 type is named "Berkshire" for the type's first owner, the Boston & Albany (B&A) Railroad, which traversed the Berkshire Mountains of Massachusetts. A few years earlier, Woodard had introduced a remarkable 2-8-2 that broke all previous records for performance and operating economy. Then came the new "A-1" 2-8-4 in 1925, which soon proved to be a landmark design Lima called "Super Power." Its big firebox, where all the energy is released, was unprecedented for a locomotive of its size. Both the area of its grate (to burn more coal per minute) and its combustion volume (to release and transfer more heat to the boiler water) broke long-standing rules. To support the heavier engine weight due to the bigger boiler, a four-wheel rear truck played a key role. A rear truck doesn't "support" a bigger back end; that's a misconception. The engine's whole equalized suspension—including the truck—supports the heavier locomotive, as a whole, to keep on-rail wheel loadings within limits.

In an extraordinary "runoff" race between a two-year-old Lima 2-8-2 and the A-1, the two competed with trains over the B&A's rugged Albany Division. The Berkshire, starting somewhat later with a somewhat heavier train, overtook the 2-8-2 on the parallel track and easily won the race hands-down.

Lima used cutting-edge marketing techniques for its day. It created the new Super Power gospel for railroads: haul your freight trains faster, and you can get more ton-mileage within a given year—and therefore you'll get more revenue in that year, with less expense per mile than older locomotives. It was a gospel preached by 1225, and it won over railroads across the country.

***

William L. Withuhn *is Curator Emeritus of the Smithsonian Institution and a member of the Brotherhood of Locomotive Engineers & Trainmen, Retired.*

CHAPTER 1

STEAM AND THE SUPER POWER REVOLUTION

On a gray day in November 1941, a group of men gathered outside the cavernous factory of the Lima Locomotive Works in Lima, Ohio. Towering beside them was a gleaming steam locomotive, a 2-8-4 type, so designated for its two leading wheels, its eight driving wheels, and its four-wheel truck under the firebox. Fresh from final assembly, it was ready for its portrait by the company photographer. Inspectors made a final check of every important component and signed an Interstate Commerce Commission Form 3 certificate, attesting that everything was in proper condition, from its huge boiler to its 69-inch driving wheels, from its brakes to its coal and water tender. A notary public witnessed the procedure.

Beautiful as it was, the machine was ordinary, just one of a dozen identical versions leaving the Lima property around that time to be delivered to the buyer in Toledo. Up to that moment it was known as Lima order number 1155 and serial number 7839, scrawled in chalk on various steel components as they came together on the shop floor. But now it carried a name and a number, painted across its flanks in pale Venetian yellow: PERE MARQUETTE 1225.

Over its eighty-year history, Lima would manufacture more than 7,500 steam locomotives. This was just another one. Or so it seemed.

◆　◆　◆

◀ Gleaming in fresh paint and buffed running gear, a completed 1225 poses outside at the Lima factory on November 4, 1941. Courtesy of John B. Corns collection.

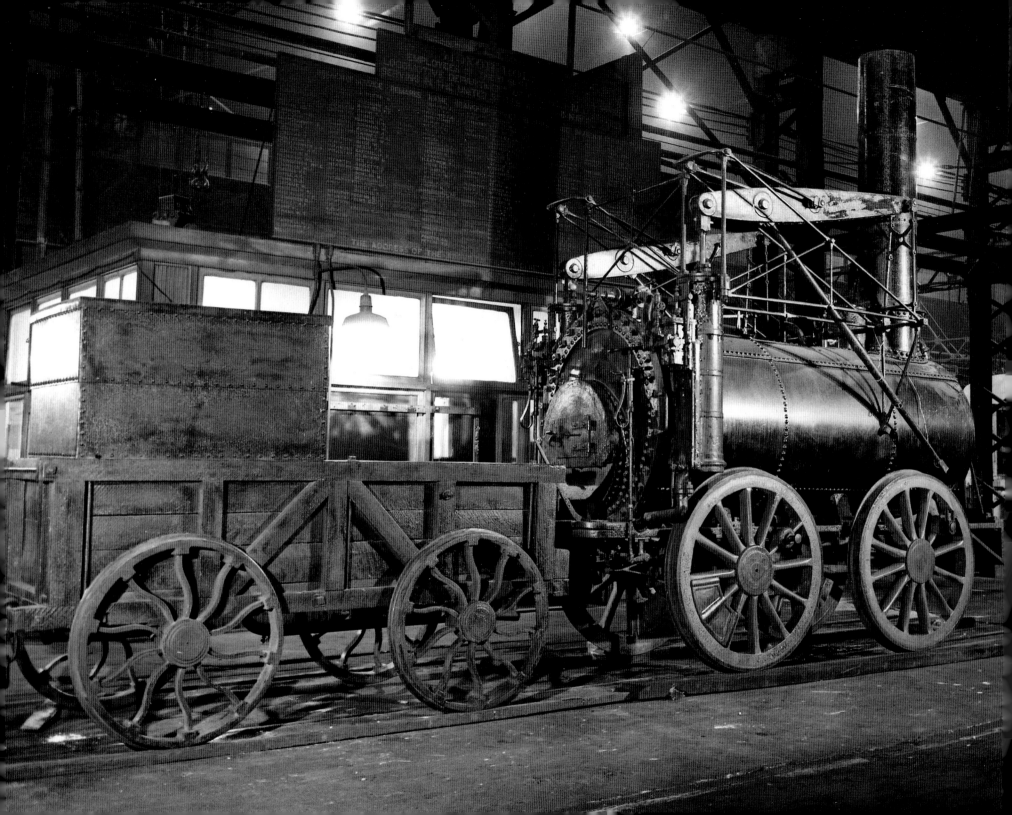

Since 1829, Americans have been mesmerized by the steam locomotive. Their first encounter came on August 8, 1829, when Horatio Allen made a trial run out of Honesdale, Pennsylvania, with a tiny four-wheel engine called the *Stourbridge Lion*. Made of wood and iron and weighing a mere 7 tons, the *Lion* was little more than a rolling teakettle, and an unsafe one at that. It never achieved any practical use.

Two successive locomotives made much better impressions. On August 28, 1830, New York manufacturer and inventor Peter Cooper successfully demonstrated his *Tom Thumb* locomotive on the fledgling Baltimore & Ohio Railroad from Ellicott's Mills, Maryland, to Baltimore. Even though the steam train was beaten by a horse-drawn railway carriage, the *Tom Thumb* proved it was practical. The outcome was more impressive on January 15, 1831, when another domestically built locomotive, the *Best Friend of Charleston*, hauled loaded cars on the South Carolina Railroad. It was the first use of steam in commercial service in the United States.

Soon, others began building steam locomotives, notably Matthias Baldwin of Philadelphia, who had success with his *Old Ironsides* of 1832. It was another odd contraption, with an ungainly 2-2-0 wheel arrangement, but it was the first successful locomotive with a horizontal boiler. Baldwin

▲ The Baltimore & Ohio built this replica of Peter Cooper's pioneering locomotive of 1830, the *Tom Thumb*. Courtesy of *Trains* magazine collection.

◄ Inventor Horatio Allen's locomotive of 1829, the *Stourbridge Lion*, poses in the Delaware & Hudson Railway's shop at Colonie, New York, in 1972. Photo by Jim Shaughnessy, courtesy of *Trains* magazine collection.

would build on the success of his engine to create the Baldwin Locomotive Works, the number one American manufacturer of steam locomotives.

If these early locomotives were mere curiosities, they also were compelling to a culture dependent on the horse. It was a fascination described elegantly by the historian John H. White: "Here was a machine that literally had fire in its belly. It roared down the track, a big clattering thing with a noisy bell and whistle. It was heavy and ponderous but cocksure: it rolled on, self-reliant and unafraid. Its only bad habits were drinking and smoking. It is no wonder, then, that thousands have been seduced by the charms and power of the steam locomotive."[1]

The public's mass adulation of steam came with the development of the 4-4-0, dubbed the American type, the most successful design of the nineteenth century. The wheel arrangement was patented in 1837 by Henry R. Campbell, chief engineer of the Philadelphia, Germantown & Norristown Railroad. Campbell's aim was to "distribute the weight of the engine upon the rails more completely."[2]

The 4-4-0 beautifully lived up to the goal. A model of balance and symmetry, it featured a deep firebox suspended between the driving wheels, feeding a boiler with a low center of gravity. It could run smoothly on any kind of track, and in the nineteenth century, track generally was crude. With an accessible boiler and valve gear, the locomotive was easy to maintain. It was also the first successful "dual service" engine, meaning it was a good choice for either passenger or freight service. It was so successful that approximately 20,000 4-4-0s were built between 1840 and 1890.

The American type became fixed in the public imagination. The 4-4-0 was the engine of the Civil War, exemplified by the Western & Atlantic's *General* and *Texas*, the key combatants in the Great Locomotive Chase through northern Georgia in 1862. Millions witnessed Abraham Lincoln's funeral train in April 1865 as it traveled from Washington, D.C., to Springfield, Illinois, behind a series of 4-4-0s. When the transcontinental railroads joined at Promontory Summit, Utah, on May 10, 1869, the attending engines were the Central Pacific's *Jupiter* and the Union Pacific's 119, both 4-4-0s. For a half-century, images of the American type were a fixture in *Harper's Weekly*,

◄ A replica of Southern Railway's *Best Friend of Charleston* of 1831 performs during a public event in Greenville, South Carolina, in July 1970. Photo by William J. Husa Jr., courtesy of *Trains* magazine collection.

Frank Leslie's Illustrated Newspaper, and other popular publications of the day.

After Promontory, the explosive growth of railroads in the late nineteenth century gradually eclipsed the capabilities of the 4-4-0. New and larger locomotives began to hold sway. The 4-4-0 begat the 4-6-0 Ten-Wheeler and the 4-4-2 Atlantic, whose larger boilers and taller driving wheels allowed for faster passenger trains. They in turn led to the standard passenger engine of the early twentieth century, the 4-6-2 Pacific. On the freight side, the 2-8-0 Consolidation dominated with its larger weight and increased tractive effort.

A breakthrough in horsepower came after the turn of the twentieth century with the ascension of the 2-8-2 Mikado, named for an order of engines Baldwin built in 1897 for the Japanese Government Railways. The Mikado came into its own in 1904 when the Northern Pacific Railway bought them in quantity from the Brooks Works of the American Locomotive Company (Alco). The 2-8-2 caught on quickly with other railroads. Like the 4-4-0 of an earlier era, its weight was perfectly balanced, this time between matched sets of drivers and

trucks. With a generous firebox and standard 63-inch drivers, the 2-8-2 became a platform for technological breakthroughs such as mechanical coal stokers and superheaters. American builders went on to construct more than 14,000 2-8-2s.

◆　　◆　　◆

The ultimate step in steam locomotive design came not from the two largest, most prominent builders—Alco and Baldwin—but from Lima Locomotive Works, a relatively small company with its roots in machinery

▲ The *General*, a classic example of the 4-4-0 American-type locomotive, as restored by Louisville & Nashville in 1959 for the centennial of the Civil War. Courtesy of *Trains* magazine collection.

◄ In an 1882 photograph taken at Lakeview, Michigan, railroaders on a work train gather around a 4-4-0 of the Detroit, Lansing & Northern, a predecessor of the *Pere Marquette*. The classic American-type engine was the last woodburner on the railroad. Courtesy of *Trains* magazine collection.

▲ The first modern freight workhorse to gain mass acceptance was the 2-8-2, exemplified by Northern Pacific 1506, built by Alco in 1904 and shown here at Duluth, Minnesota, in 1955. *Courtesy of Louis A. Marre collection.*

manufacturing. Formed in 1869 as Carnes, Harper & Company by five partners from Upper Sandusky, Ohio, the firm purchased a factory in the town of Lima and went on to make sawmill machinery, threshing machines, traction engines, and stationary steam engines. It was incorporated as Lima Machine Works in 1876.

Expansion plans led company managers to consider the lumber industry, which was thriving in nearby Michigan. Eventually the company encountered a lumberman named Ephraim Shay of Haring, Michigan. Shay was also an inventor and had been working on the problem of transporting logs to the mill using a new kind of small locomotive that wouldn't tear up the lightweight track and steep grades common to forest land without extensive earthwork. His experimenting led to a design incorporating a small boiler that could convey power directly to flexible trucks under the locomotive, without conventional rods and driving wheels.

Shay turned to Lima to see if it could push his idea forward. The company was enthusiastic, and quickly perfected Shay's prototype by developing a geared mechanism that delivered power by means of a combination journal box, line shaft, and driving pinion gears on each axle of the engine and tender. Dubbed "Shays," the powerful, slow-moving little locomotives could dig in under any kind of track conditions. Soon, Lima was producing hundreds of Shays and shipping them all over the world.

Success with the Shays led Lima to make a profound change of course in 1915, reorganizing the company to concentrate on rod engines and establishing a new design group led by William E. Woodard, a brilliant young engineer recently recruited from Alco. Woodard soon was named vice president of engineering. He moved quickly to make his mark.

Woodard had become convinced that the steam locomotive's performance was limited only by its design. Shippers demanded faster service and heavier trains. The conventional freight train of the era was a slow drag, characterized by a 2-8-2 lugging across a division at 15 to 20 miles per hour. Nationally, the average train speed was a mere 11.5 miles per hour.

The problem was that builders couldn't make ever-larger versions of rigid-frame models such as 2-8-2s and 2-10-2s, due to the limitations of bridges, clearances, and other factors of the physical plant; these machines were simply becoming too heavy. Neither were ever-larger articulated Mallet compound-style locomotives the answer. These employed two sets of drivers under a single boiler and used steam twice, first with high-pressure steam in the rear cylinders, then exhausting it through huge low-pressure cylinders in front. The best Mallets—notably the 2-8-8-2—could pull like crazy. But they were slow.

For Woodard, the answer lay in reinventing the steam locomotive. If speeds needed to go up,

Inventor Ephraim Shay. Courtesy of Allen County Historical Society.

▲ Typical of Lima's famed Shay geared locomotive is No. 73, a two-truck engine built for Ohio's Kelley Island Lime & Transport Company. *Courtesy of Trains magazine collection.*

locomotives would require more powerful boilers and higher horsepower. To achieve those goals, a locomotive's weight would have to be redistributed. This led to Woodard's and Lima's central innovation: a substantially larger firebox matched with a four-wheel trailing truck.

Sound as Lima's thinking was, skeptical railroad companies had to be convinced in the field, especially when the innovation was coming from the number 3 builder. Lima would have to build a demonstrator engine, and it needed a railroad as a sponsor. In the summer of 1921, Woodard found a partner, the New York Central (NYC), which was eager to get more production out of its large fleets of H-7 class 2-8-2 Mikados and L-1 class 4-8-2 Mohawks.

The result was a "super" 2-8-2, H-10 No. 8000, lettered for NYC subsidiary Michigan Central. Although the new locomotive was similar to other NYC 2-8-2s in overall weight and proportion, it was packed with Lima's innovations. They included a substantially larger firebox grate area of 66.4

square feet, about 10 percent larger than the standard H-7; improved superheaters that boosted heating-surface area by 53 percent; a front-end throttle built into the superheater header at the front of the engine; the addition of arch brick in the firebox, which redirected burning gas to the rear of the firebox before it moved forward through the flues; a trailing-truck booster engine to help start a train; and lightweight side rods made of higher-strength steel.

Rolled out in June 1922, 8000 weighed 334,000 pounds, only marginally more than a standard 2-8-2. But in trials the new locomotive hauled heavier trains while using less fuel. In a test conducted between Detroit and Toledo, 8000 easily pulled a 138-car train, which, at 9,254 tons, was very heavy for the era. Test results showed the H-10 developed approximately 35 percent more drawbar horsepower than a conventional 2-8-2, with much higher boiler efficiency. After six weeks of tests, the NYC was sufficiently impressed to order seventy-five H-10s from Lima, including 8000. The railroad ultimately ordered 300 of the model, of which 115 were from Lima and the rest from Alco.

▼ Official builder's photo of New York Central 8000, the first Super Power 2-8-2, built by Lima in June 1922. Courtesy of *Trains* magazine collection.

◆   ◆   ◆

But the H-10 wasn't enough. Woodard and his design team wanted to build an ever better locomotive—this time from scratch. The American economy was picking up steam, impelled largely by the growing auto industry centered in Michigan and the Midwest. The auto plants were also producing motor trucks that were beginning to compete for fast freight haulage. The railroads needed more power and speed. Woodward wanted a machine that incorporated all the elements of the Lima gospel, and then some. It needed to generate huge volumes of steam and boiler horsepower. It would require the new four-wheel trailing truck to support the firebox. It needed to take advantage of the latest improvements in appliances such as feedwater heaters and superheaters. To achieve all this, Lima indicated it would create an entirely new wheel arrangement: the 2-8-4. The company would call this new breed of locomotive Super Power.

In September 1924, Lima began construction of a stock 2-8-4, an investment of $116,800, or about $1.6 million in current dollars. No

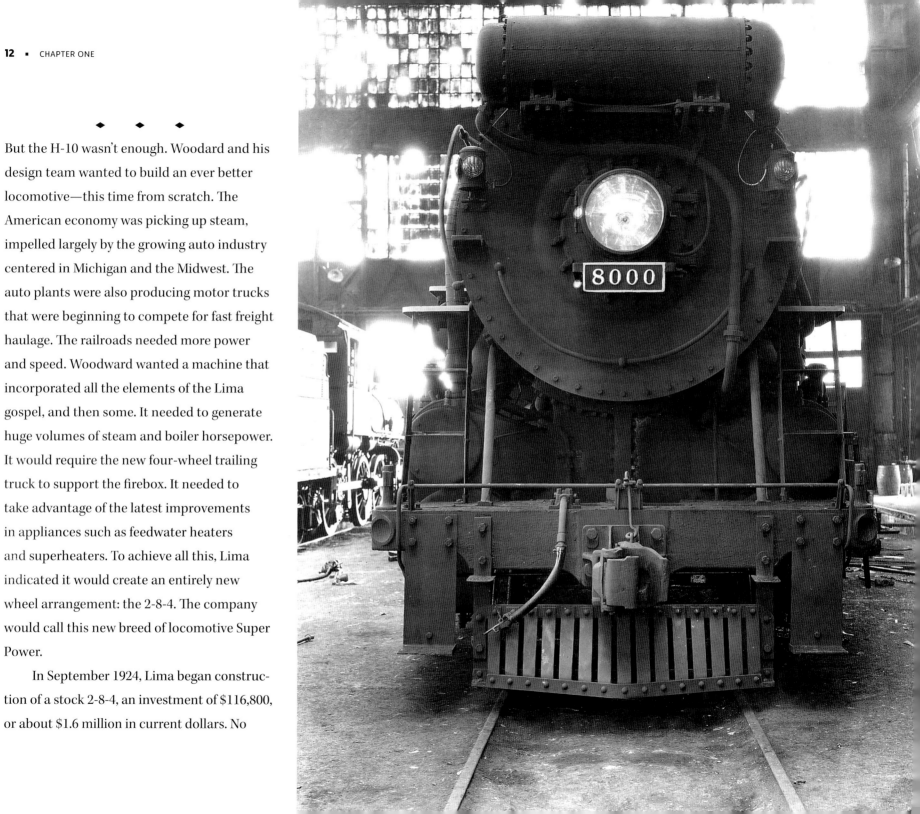

railroad would sign on as a full sponsor, but once again the NYC agreed to give the new locomotive a try. By January 1925, Lima was calling the new engine the A-1 and dispatched it to NYC subsidiary Boston & Albany (B&A). The B&A possessed a challenging main line across western Massachusetts through the Berkshire Hills—the perfect place to put the A-1 through its paces.

The following February, Lima president J. S. Coffin unveiled the A-1 at a ceremony in Lima, calling it "the finest piece of machinery I've ever seen." He had reason to boast. The A-1 featured a long list of major improvements:

- a firebox with 100 square feet of grate area, a record for a rigid-frame locomotive
- a four-wheel articulated trailing truck
- a new ashpan design that improved airflow through the firebox
- cast-steel cylinders with integrated steam passages
- operating boiler pressure of 240 psi, 20 percent higher than the H-10's 200 psi
- new tandem main rods, reducing wear on the highly stressed main crankpins.

The A-1 cut an imposing figure, especially on its front end. By placing the Elesco feedwater atop the smokebox and matching it with a pair of cross-compound air compressors mounted on the pilot deck, Lima created an elegant, enduring look that would be become a trademark not only of its 2-8-4 but of other Lima locomotives to come.

Although the trade press initially called the 2-8-4 a "Lima" out of deference to its builder, the name "Berkshire" began to catch on once it went to work on the B&A on March 28, 1925. Outfitted with a small wooden shelter on the pilot deck to protect technicians, the locomotive also hauled the NYC's dynamometer car, described as "a railroad laboratory on wheels." Various steam gauges, thermometers, and other indicators were placed at key points on the locomotive to measure the performance of cylinders, superheaters, the booster engine, the feedwater heater, and even the weights of the water and coal consumed.

◀ Smokebox view of Lima's experimental 2-8-2, New York Central 8000, inside the Lima factory. *Courtesy of Trains magazine collection.*

The NYC ran useful test runs between March 28 and April 15 over the B&A's Albany Division between Selkirk Yard, near Albany, and Washington, Massachusetts, 60 miles of tortuous curves and a heavy eastbound grade. The test period included winter and spring weather, obliging the A-1 to perform on track that was variously icy, wet, or dry. The engine ended up making nine useful test runs.

The trials were an unqualified success, as demonstrated by this account of a single outing, by Richard J. Cook:

Unquestionably the most dramatic test occurred April 14, 1925. At 10:57 that morning, No. 190, a class H-10 2-8-2 Mikado type, steamed eastbound from the Selkirk Yard with a manifest (fast freight) consisting of 46 cars aggregating 1,691 tons. Almost one hour later, at 11:44 A.M., the A-1 with the dynamometer car in tow led a string of 54 cars from the same yard with a total of 2,296 tons. As the A-1 passed the yard limit sign, she put her shoulder to the hard eastbound climb

through the Berkshires. Not far ahead, No. 190 with a lighter train made good time without any undue delays. Steadily the A-1 narrowed the gap.

At Chatham, No. 190 was switched to the outside track, and moments later, the A-1 came into the block. In a matter of minutes, the A-1 pulled up to the caboose and was running side by side on the parallel track. Between East Chatham and Canaan, the most difficult portion of the line came into view, a section with numerous curves

▲ Still equipped with a cage for technicians, the A-1 hauls the Milwaukee Road's *Pioneer Limited* over the Short Line Bridge in Minneapolis on October 24, 1925. Courtesy of *Trains* magazine collection.

◄ First of the breed: Lima's A-1 2-8-4 of 1925, the first engine to feature the larger firebox and supporting four-wheel trailing truck so critical to the Super Power concept. Courtesy of *Trains* magazine collection.

and a heavy grade. This didn't hold back the A-1: she kept pace with the 190, then overtook her car by car. . . . The 2-8-4 rolled into North Adams Junction at 2:02 P.M., just 10 minutes ahead of the Mikado.[3]

The A-1 proved what it came to prove. In the April 14 run, the A-1 had handled 26 percent more tonnage in fifty-seven fewer minutes across the same miles as the H-10, all while setting records for boiler efficiency, drawbar horsepower, and consumption of coal and water as measured by the test engineers riding along.

The A-1 and the Super Power doctrine caused a stir throughout railroading. Lima sent the A-1 on a barnstorming tour of several railroads, including the Illinois Central, Milwaukee Road, Missouri Pacific, and Chesapeake & Ohio (C&O). In the Milwaukee Road demonstration, the A-1 worked the railroad's La Crosse and Illinois Divisions, including a stint on the railroad's *Pioneer Limited* over the 421 miles between Chicago and Minneapolis, successfully keeping to the train's tight schedule.

Perhaps more momentous were tests on the C&O's mountainous Allegheny Division out of Hinton, West Virginia, where the A-1 performed for mechanical representatives from the C&O, the Erie, the Nickel Plate, and a regional railroad in Michigan called the Pere Marquette. All four companies were owned by Oris P. and Mantis J. Van Sweringen of Cleveland, brothers and real-estate magnates who had decided to establish a big stake in railroading. The Van Sweringens had a reputation for turning their railroads into first-class properties. It's no exaggeration to say they wanted the best locomotives money could buy, even for the Pere Marquette, their smallest holding. After watching the A-1, their mechanical officers came away impressed.

▶ In an aerial photo taken near the end of the steam era, the Lima Locomotive Works complex dominates the southwest side of Lima. At lower right is Lima's Main Street administrative office. Photo by Lima Locomotive Works, courtesy of *Trains* magazine collection.

Courtesy of Allen County Historical Society.

LIMA'S WIZARD OF STEAM

William E. Woodard brought his Super Power locomotive design to the railroads of America, revolutionizing their concept of how freight-train speed related to economy and earnings.

Woodard was born in Utica, New York, in 1873. He received an engineering degree in 1896 at Cornell University's Sibley School, the most prestigious university engineering department in the United States at the time. Woodard next worked at Cramp's Shipyard, a large firm in Philadelphia, and soon after at Baldwin Locomotive Works (BLW). He left BLW to join the Dickson Manufacturing Company in Scranton, Pennsylvania, and later the Schenectady Locomotive Works. The Dickson and Schenectady works both were parts of the consolidated American Locomotive Company, later known as Alco.

While at Alco, Woodard became a close associate of Francis Cole, then America's most accomplished locomotive designer. During World War I, Woodard served with the United States Railroad Administration (USRA) helping design the standardized locomotives of the war years, engines that soon became favorite designs on many railroads. For example, Southern

Railway Ps-4 No. 1401, displayed at the Smithsonian Institution in Washington, D.C., is of a class based on a USRA Pacific.

Woodard later became chief consulting engineer to Lima, Franklin Railway Supply, the Superheater Company, and American Arch Company—all parts of a conglomerate put together by Joel Coffin and Sam Allen beginning in 1916. Coffin and Allen then owned part of Franklin but had bigger intentions.

At the conclusion of World War I, they went after Woodard. His son George kept the nearly yearlong correspondence: his father played a tactful waiting game. By the end of it, the elder Woodard had secured a bigger salary from Lima, a vice presidential position, and agreement that he could stay permanently in New York (as his wife, Phoebe, demanded), with a design office in a building next to Grand Central Terminal. He commuted to Lima frequently, most likely via the Pennsylvania Railroad.

In the locomotive business, patent suits were common. Woodard was masterful in his testimony during such suits, the senior partner of Lima's law firm often said. Woodard's answers were always crisp and "never gave anything away" to the opposition. He was vastly

better in understanding the technology at issue than any patent attorney.

Woodard's last major project was the poppet-valve gear and double-ported valves for the Pennsylvania Railroad's streamlined T1 4-4-4-4 duplex-drive passenger locomotive, for which he set up a semisecret team of designers working in Baltimore known as the Balmar Company, with a staff Woodard personally selected from the Coffin and Allen group. It was a "skunk works" for steam, years before Lockheed Aircraft conceived of the name.

At his death in 1942, Woodard was at work on a proposed 2-6-6-6 design without the excess weights-on-axles that plagued the Chesapeake & Ohio's Allegheny type of the same wheel arrangement, with a "double-Belpaire" firebox providing greater furnace volume for yet more combustion efficiency and higher drawbar power with better fuel economy.

Today's high-horsepower road diesels from General Electric and Electro-Motive pull scheduled freight faster than forty years ago or even twenty years ago. Woodard's Lima gospel of higher speed for higher productivity lives on.

—*William L. Withuhn*

CHAPTER 2

The Rise of the Pere Marquette

The Pere Marquette (PM) could be called Michigan's own railroad. Its history mirrors that of the entire state. The railroad spread out across the Lower Peninsula in the late nineteenth century, linking port cities and farm towns and vast forests. Its predecessor companies were built to haul fruit, grain, and, most of all, lumber. Its distinctive name was iconic, derived from the town of Pere Marquette and the river it straddled on the shore of Lake Michigan. True to Michigan's unique geography, it quickly established a network of railroad carferries.

Michigan's earliest pioneers found forests as vast as any in the country. The most desirable product was white pine; records indicate many trees were as much as 200 feet high and 8 feet in diameter. Pine was lumbered generally north of a line from Muskegon to Saginaw. South of the line the principal product was hardwoods. The peak of Michigan's timber production came in 1889–90, when 5.5 billion board feet of lumber, mostly pine, was hauled out of the woods.

Rooted in those forests, the Pere Marquette family tree was a jumble of seventy-eight ancestral railroads, the earliest of which, the Flint & Fentonville, opened for business in 1863. Their most common shared trait was financial failure.

By the end of the century, they had coalesced into three main carriers. The Detroit, Grand Rapids & Western (DGR&W) extended from Detroit westward through Lansing to Grand Rapids, with branch lines reaching into farm country between Grand Ledge and Grand Rapids. The Flint & Pere Marquette (F&PM) linked Toledo with Flint and Saginaw, and extended its main line northwesterly across the state to Ludington, the new name for the town of Pere Marquette. The F&PM also operated a network of narrow-gauge lines fanning out across the "Thumb"—the east-central region of the state that defines the Lower Peninsula's mitten shape—acquired from the Port Huron & Northwestern. In the western part of the state, the Chicago & West Michigan (C&WM) extended from the southern terminus of La Crosse, Indiana, northward through New Buffalo to Grand Rapids, then far north to Traverse City, Charlevoix, and Petoskey. At its south end, the C&WM intersected every major eastern trunk line entering Chicago.

The timber didn't last long. By the turn of the twentieth century, Michigan's productive forests were largely gone, eliminating lumber as an important source of rail traffic. It was at this point the twentieth-century version of the PM came together with the January 1, 1900, consolidation of the F&PM, DGR&W, and

▶ In a turn-of-the-century postcard view, a pair of Pere Marquette trains meet at the Edmore depot, junction of several Pere Marquette branches northeast of Grand Rapids. Courtesy of *Trains* magazine collection.

▲ The crew of an ancient Pere Marquette 0-4-0 poses with their engine deep in timber country at Sigma, Michigan, northeast of Cadillac. Courtesy of *Trains* magazine collection.

C&WM. The new company linked most of the most important cities in the Lower Peninsula, but its prospects were limited without getting directly into Chicago.

New management in 1903 solved this problem, pushing the PM into Chicago via a trackage-rights agreement with the New York Central's (NYC's) subsidiary Lake Shore & Michigan Southern (LS&MS). The PM built a new line from New Buffalo south twenty-one miles to Porter, Indiana, where it connected with the LS&MS. In Chicago, PM passenger trains accessed Grand Central Station via a separate trackage rights agreement with the Chicago Terminal Transfer Railroad, a predecessor of the Baltimore & Ohio Chicago Terminal.

Management instability still plagued the PM, however, and between 1904 and 1907 the railroad's ownership was traded off among a number of railroads, including the Cincinnati, Hamilton & Dayton; the Baltimore & Ohio; and the Erie. Continued financial weakness triggered receiverships in 1907 and 1912. This led to the creation of a new version of the railroad, the Pere Marquette Railway, incorporated in 1917 to absorb the former PM.

Problematic as the PM continued to be, its strategic location gradually came into focus as Detroit's automobile industry took off after World War I. With its key main lines extending south from Detroit to Toledo and northward to Flint and Saginaw, the PM offered ideal corridors for hauling coal, other raw materials, and auto parts into the Detroit area, and finished automobiles out. The railroad's carferry services out of Ludington on the shore of Lake Michigan offered a natural bridge route between Buffalo and the West, giving shippers a chance to bypass the congestion of Chicago.

◆　◆　◆

These advantages became obvious to O.P. and M.J. Van Sweringen, bachelor brothers who had made a fortune in suburban Cleveland development after the turn of the twentieth century. Oris, the older brother, was born in 1879; Mantis was born in 1881. The boys grew up as strict Congregationalists in a working-class family of six children on Cleveland's east side. They've been described as inseparable, with O.P. generally cast as the "thinker" and M.J. as the "doer." Together, the "Vans," as they were known, dabbled in various small businesses until they settled on what they liked best: real estate.

The Van Sweringens flourished as developers, making their first big splash in 1905 with Shaker Heights, a planned community built on a large tract on the southeast edge of Cleveland. The success of the town depended on construction of a high-speed rapid-transit line to downtown Cleveland. The downtown connection—and their association with NYC president Alfred H. Smith—led to their crowning real-estate achievement, completion in 1930 of the massive Terminal Tower complex at the Public Square. The project became the Van Sweringens' new headquarters and featured offices, retail space, a hotel, and the city's main railroad station.

The Van Sweringens' interests led them inevitably toward railroading. They had become leading exponents of leveraged financing, using holding companies to extend their control of business after business. In 1916, the brothers acquired the New York, Chicago & St. Louis Railroad, known as the Nickel Plate Road (NKP), which had been spun off by the NYC under

Oris P. Van Sweringen. Courtesy of *Trains* magazine collection.

Mantis J. Van Sweringen. Courtesy of *Trains* magazine collection.

antitrust pressure. In a pattern to be followed with other railroads, and following advice from Smith, the owners invested heavily in the NKP, dramatically upgrading its operations and infrastructure.

Other railroad acquisitions soon followed. In 1922, the brothers expanded the NKP by acquiring the Lake Erie & Western and the Toledo, St. Louis & Western (known as the "Cloverleaf") and turning them into one large system. With this, the brothers could market the NKP as a bridge route from Buffalo to Chicago and St. Louis, an alternative to big trunk lines such as the NYC and the Pennsylvania Railroad. By 1924, their empire had grown exponentially with the acquisition of the Erie, the Chesapeake & Ohio (C&O), and the PM. Separate attempts in 1926 and 1929 to merge these properties into a unified system were blocked by the Interstate Commerce Commission (ICC), so in 1929 the Vans brought them under the umbrella of a new holding company called the Alleghany Corporation.

Although smaller than the other properties, the PM was a key part of

▶ The Terminal Tower complex, the signature real-estate achievement of the Van Sweringen brothers, sprawls across downtown Cleveland in this aerial photo taken shortly before the terminal's grand opening in 1930.
Courtesy of Herbert H. Harwood Jr. collection.

Alleghany's portfolio. For one thing, the latest previous iteration of PM management had vastly improved the railroad's fortunes. Between 1913 and 1923, the company grew operating revenues 150 percent, from more than $16 million to nearly $46 million. More important to the Van Sweringens, net income over the same period had ballooned from a $7.2 million deficit to a profit of $5.2 million. For the first time in the PM's history, the railroad was a going business.

The potential of Michigan's automotive industry burnished the PM's prospects. The Van Sweringens and their mentor, NYC's Smith, for some time had coveted the PM's connections with the C&O in Toledo and the NKP in Chicago. The Toledo link was especially valuable to the brothers' largest railroad holding, the C&O. "We decided the Chesapeake & Ohio should have additional outlets for its coal shippers," wrote O.P. Van Sweringen. "Industrial Michigan seemed to fill the bill, and so we bought into the Pere Marquette."[1]

The Van Sweringens' influence over the PM would be short-lived, however. They

briefly sustained the dramatic growth of their empire with the acquisition of the Missouri Pacific (MoPac)–Texas & Pacific system, as well as the much smaller Chicago & Eastern Illinois (C&EI). Control of MoPac also gave them a half interest in the Denver & Rio Grande Western, which, in theory, could have

▲ The first AMC-designed Berkshire: an engine crew inspects Nickel Plate 2-8-4 No. 700 shortly after its delivery from Alco in 1930. Courtesy of *Trains* magazine collection.

◀ The Advisory Mechanical Committee's first creation was the C&O T-1 2-10-4, which led directly to the development of the 2-8-4. Here, T-1 No. 3006 hustles a 5,000-ton freight train south of Linworth, Ohio. Photo by Glenn Grabill Jr., courtesy of *Trains* magazine collection.

extended the Van Sweringens' holdings nearly to the West Coast.

But by the early 1930s the Depression was cutting deeply into the Vans' fortunes, just as the MoPac acquisition was taking effect. The PM's stock price had risen from $61 to $260 in the five years 1925–29; it had fallen to $130 by September 30, 1930. In 1931, the price slipped to $4. Bankruptcy followed in 1933 for MoPac and the C&EI, and revenues sank on the other member railroads. It is generally accepted that only the C&O, its financial strength rooted in coal, kept the whole empire afloat. Further refinancing in 1935 from Indiana millionaire George M. Ball and a new holding company called Midamerica Corporation brought some relief. Alas, both Van Sweringen brothers died within a year of each other, M.J. on December 12, 1935, and O.P. on November 23, 1936. For at least another generation, though, their names remained linked to the railroads they briefly owned.

◆   ◆   ◆

The Van Sweringens always built big. They created a town out of vacant land and turned it into Cleveland's toniest suburb.

▶ Little brother to the Berkshires: one of the Pere Marquette's ubiquitous 2-8-2s is ready for service at the railroad's Detroit engine terminal, beneath the Ambassador Bridge, in 1947. Photo by Robert A. Hadley, courtesy of *Trains* magazine collection.

They transformed the city's downtown with the grandiose Terminal Tower complex. And they left a legacy of investing in physical assets, a philosophy that led to the transformation of all the railroads they owned. The Van Sweringens upgraded track. They built new bridges. They modernized and expanded classification yards and shops, including the PM's principal maintenance terminal at Wyoming on the southwest side of Grand Rapids. And together, their various companies fielded some of the most successful steam locomotives of all time.

To ensure they would have superior motive power, the Van Sweringens' roads in 1929 organized the Advisory Mechanical Committee (AMC), based in Cleveland and pooling the member companies' best mechanical talent. Although AMC designs were not identical from railroad to railroad, there were basic similarities across all AMC engines. The committee was influenced significantly by the Super Power revolution launched by William E. Woodard and his Lima design team. Representatives of the AMC roads had already seen firsthand what Lima's A-1 2-8-4 could do on the C&O.

The AMC began its work with a project for the C&O to design an ideal locomotive to haul coal from Russell, Kentucky, to Toledo. The goal was to make a 2-10-4 that boasted the speed and boiler capacity of the 2-8-4 but also had enough power to obviate any need for helper engines in starting a heavy coal train. Working with Woodard and Lima, the C&O introduced the T-1 class 2-10-4, a tremendously successful engine whose design rested on four key components: 69-inch driving wheels, a 34-inch piston stroke, a boiler that could deliver 15 percent more horsepower than the rated horsepower of the cylinders, and a factor of adhesion of 4.07. ("Factor of adhesion" is a formula devised to measure the effectiveness of a locomotive's contact between driving wheel and rail; ideally, the engine weight on drivers should be approximately four times its tractive effort, which is a theoretical measure of force at the driving wheels, measured in pounds. A factor of adhesion of less than four, and the drivers will easily slip.)

The T-1 was a beautiful expression of the Super Power philosophy: ample power for starting, and ample horsepower at high speed. But the AMC didn't confine the success of the

◀ One of the first Pere Marquette 2-8-4s, N-1 No. 1203, poses for a publicity photo near Plymouth, Michigan. New automobile frames are visible behind the first three boxcars. Photo by Chesapeake & Ohio Railway; courtesy of John B. Corns collection.

design to the 2-10-4. When the NKP called on the committee in 1933 to develop a new fleet of engines capable of supporting more demanding freight schedules, the AMC returned to the 2-8-4 Berkshire type. Essentially, the designers scaled down a T-1 by one set of driving wheels but retained its four key characteristics: the 69-inch drivers, the 115 percent boiler, the 34-inch stroke, and the excellent factor of adhesion.

The result was the S-class 2-8-4, soon to become one of the most effective steam locomotive designs. The first fifteen NKP Berkshires were purchased from Alco and constructed at the builder's huge works in Schenectady, New York. The engines were numbered 700 to 714 and began service in late 1934. Beautifully proportioned, the 700s included a number of components that would become familiar to engines on other Van Sweringen roads: the headlight centered on the smokebox, an outside-bearing pony truck, a Delta trailing truck, spoked drivers, and cross-compound air pumps mounted behind shields on the pilot deck.

The Berkshires wowed the NKP's

▶ Its crew ready to board, N-4 1204 rides the turntable inside the full-circle roundhouse at Wyoming, Michigan, in September 1943. Courtesy of C&O Historical Society collection.

operating department. Each 2-8-4 developed more than 64,000 pounds of tractive effort, showing they could rapidly accelerate even the heaviest trains, allowing the railroad to toss aside the tonnage-rating tables used to match locomotives with trains. The S-class boilers produced prodigious amounts of steam, a blessing to engine crews. Their driving wheels were counterbalanced so effectively that wear on track was significantly reduced. NKP historian John A. Rehor put the impact of the Berks in perspective: "In its new 2-8-4, the NKP had a flawless powerhouse that it would reorder, without basic modification, five times in the next 15 years."[2]

PM managers must have been envious of what was happening on the NKP. By the mid-1930s, the PM was getting by with what could only be called a second-class locomotive fleet. The heavy lifting on freight trains was provided by fifty-five dual-service MK-class Mikado 2-8-2s, most of them built before 1920, and fifteen SF-class 2-10-2s, known as the Santa Fe type, all of them purchased in 1918. The most that could be said about these drag-era locomotives is that they were reliable.

The PM's roster of passenger engines was even more antiquated, although the PM never put much emphasis on this part of its business. By the 1930s, most of its passenger schedules were protected by twenty-seven Pacific-type 4-6-2s, some of them positively quaint: fifteen of the engines were built in 1914 or earlier. The railroad bought another twelve medium-size Pacifics from Alco in 1921.

One thing the PM's mechanical department had going for it was membership in the AMC, giving it access to the performance statistics of the NKP 2-8-4s. As the Depression eased and Detroit's industrial capacity began to revive, train tonnages and customer expectations went up, pushing the PM's creaky old engines to the breaking point. Only a new class of freight locomotive could keep the railroad competitive, and the NKP seemed to have the ticket.

◆   ◆   ◆

A small railroad like the PM would never attract the publicity afforded the NKP, but its decision to buy 2-8-4s that were near carbon copies of the NKP S-class engines proved to be momentous

▶ The Wyoming shops sprawl across the countryside in an aerial photo taken shortly after steam was retired. Highlights include the roundhouse, the giant repair shops immediately beyond it, and the new diesel shop in the foreground. Several stored Berkshires can be seen on tracks leading to the concrete coaling tower at center-left. Courtesy of C&O Historical Society collection.

on its own scale. The new PM engines would revolutionize the railroad, giving it the chance to throw off the yoke of its slow, underpowered fleet and compete with the kind of service that big industrial shippers were demanding as the national economy improved. Modern power would help the PM cement its reputation as a bridge carrier.

The Berkshire era on the PM began in 1937 with the purchase from Lima of fifteen N-class locomotives, Nos. 1201–1215, recorded by the builder as order No. 1143. They were slightly larger than the NKP 2-8-4s, with 26-by-34–inch cylinders (versus the NKP's 25-by-34–inch) and 7,600 pounds heavier, at 436,500 pounds. Each Berkshire developed more than 69,000 pounds of tractive effort. The tender capacities were the same: 22 tons of coal, 22,000 gallons of water. Nos. 1211–1215 were enhanced with trailing-truck boosters. The most obvious visual differentiator for the PM engines was the use of an elegant boiler-tube pilot compared with the NKP's utilitarian horizontal slat style. The PM engines also followed the NKP style in placing the steam dome ahead of the sandbox, a break from traditional design.

The PM's huge new locomotives could not roam the entire system. Bridge and track restrictions on the PM's many branch lines and secondary routes confined the 2-8-4s to the key main lines between Chicago and Detroit via Grand Rapids, and between Toledo and Saginaw. The restrictions were of little matter, though—these main lines carried the vast majority of the PM's traffic.

Although the 1200s technically were designed to be used in dual service, most were never equipped with steam lines to heat passenger cars, and they could not be used on passenger trains. The main reason was the engines' size: a bridge at the throat of the Fort Street Union Depot in Detroit would not support the 2-8-4's weight, and Chicago's Grand Central Station also imposed clearance restrictions.

Home for the PM's Berkshires was the sprawling shop complex at Wyoming. Built in 1905 to combine previous shops serving the DGR&W at Ionia, the F&PM at Saginaw, and the C&WM at Grand Rapids, Wyoming grew quickly to include an erecting shop, boiler shop, blacksmith

◄ Lineup of three Pere Marquette 2-8-4s under construction at Lima in the fall of 1941; 1216 is displaying its open smokebox door. Photo by Lima Locomotive Works, courtesy of John B. Corns collection.

shop, and twenty-four-stall engine house. In 1911, the engine house was replaced with a forty-two-stall full-circle roundhouse. Under Van Sweringen ownership, Wyoming in 1923 underwent a massive upgrade to include a new, larger erecting bay; new car repair shops; a new cinder pit; and lengthening of twenty-two of the forty-two roundhouse stalls to accommodate the 2-8-2s and 2-10-2s.

The railroad maintained other important maintenance terminals in Saginaw, New Buffalo, Plymouth, Flint, St. Thomas (Ontario), and Detroit, where it shared the Twenty-First Street roundhouse along the Detroit River with the Wabash and Baltimore & Ohio. But Wyoming was the heart of the railroad, where three generations of boilermakers, blacksmiths, machinists, and other skilled workers practiced the art of keeping PM steam locomotives on the road.

Lima promotional copy was emphatic about the advantages of the new PM engines: "The increasing demands for quick deliveries on the part of shippers have brought about an entirely new concept of the handling of freight. Today fast freight schedules must parallel those of fast passenger trains." The newest member of the Berkshire club quickly proved that to be true. Dramatic changes in PM's freight service began almost the moment the first engine of the order, No. 1201, was shipped from Lima on September 13, 1937. The engines promptly were deployed in service on the Detroit, Chicago, and Toledo Divisions, accompanied at first by mechanical department employees who tested the engines and helped crews learn how to operate them.

◆　◆　◆

The Berkshires took the PM by storm. To measure the impact of the 2-8-4s, consider freight-train tonnages and timekeeping between Detroit and Grand Rapids. Before the Berkshires, the MK-class 2-8-2s could manage 1,750-ton trains and the SF-class 2-10-2s slightly larger 2,000-ton trains, dictated by their ability to haul these trains up the ruling westbound grade of 1.15 percent from Plymouth to South Lyon without requiring a helper locomotive. Eastbound, the 2-8-2s could manage 2,100-ton trains and the 2-10-2s up to 2,300-ton trains up the 1.10 percent ruling grade from Wyoming to Elmdale, again without a helper.

▶ A completed N-1 boiler awaits the installation of external parts on the Lima shop floor in a photo taken October 10, 1941. Photo by Lima Locomotive Works, courtesy of John B. Corns collection.

1155-20
10-11-41

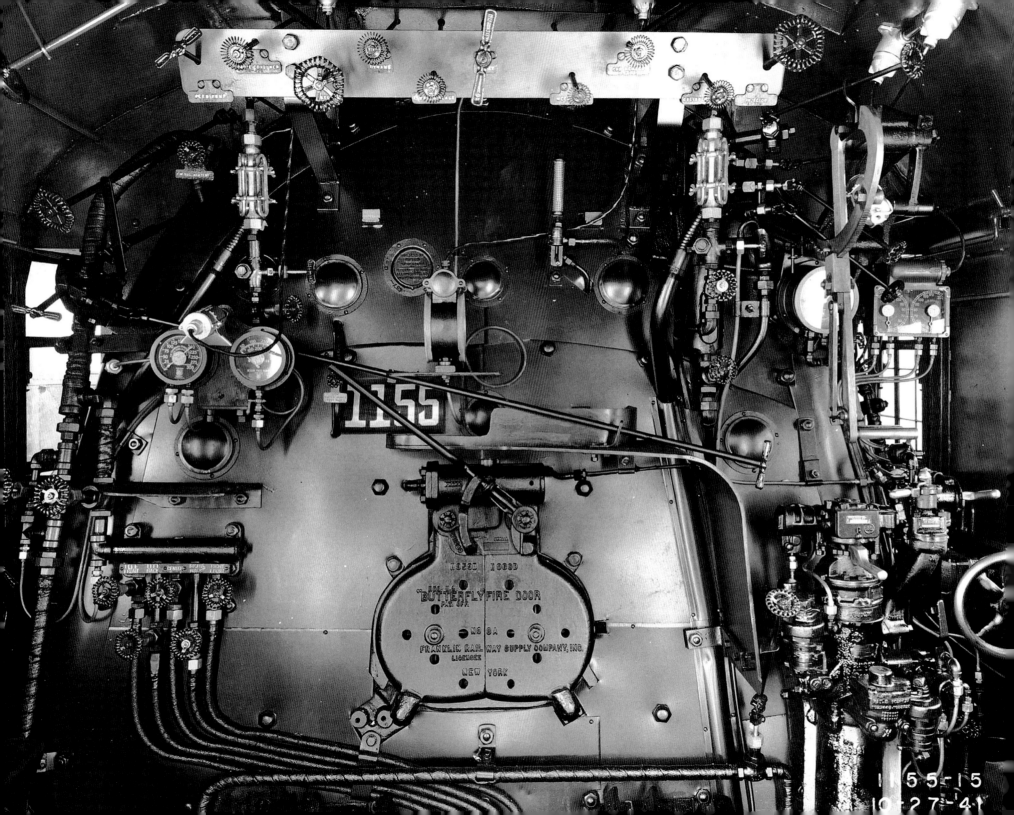

The 1200s could easily handle another 1,000 tons per train in either direction. They could get an average fifty-car train over the railroad at sustained speeds of 50 to 60 miles per hour and generally average 30 miles per hour across the breadth of the system, allowing for stops and servicing.

The PM showed off its new power in 1939 with the launch of a new Detroit to Chicago service called the *Overnighter*. These trains, numbered 40 eastbound and 41 westbound, handled the usual overhead traffic and carload shipments, but the railroad also took aim at the less-than-carload (LCL) service increasingly going to truckers. For eastbound traffic, the railroad promised that LCL shipments arriving at Chicago's Clearing Yard by 4:30 P.M. would depart on train 40 at 7 P.M. and arrive Detroit at 5:30 A.M. Westbound, shipments delivered to Detroit's Boat Yard by 4 P.M. would depart on train 41 at 5:45 P.M., with a 3 A.M. arrival at Chicago.

◄ Cab interior of a brand-new N-1. Key components include the notched grapevine throttle at upper right, the Franklin reverse wheel at lower right, an adjacent brake stand, and, on the opposite side of the cab, a series of five valves to control the stoker engine. Photo by Lima Locomotive Works, courtesy of John B. Corns collection.

▼ Engineer's-side view of a completed 1225, in the customary formal rods-down pose, ready for delivery on November 4, 1941. Photo by Lima Locomotive Works, courtesy of John B. Corns collection.

A still-shiny 1225 makes one of its first revenue trips as it rolls through Delray Junction in Detroit with an outbound freight on November 29, 1941. Photo by Lynn E. Taylor, courtesy of Steam Railroading Institute collection.

The *Overnighters* nearly matched the over-the-road performance of the PM's passenger trains. Indeed, the railroad advertised the freight service in full-page ads in its public timetables. A May 1940 report showed that train 41 averaged 37.6 miles per hour over the entire distance from Detroit to Chicago, remarkably fast for the steam era. The 1942 timetable shows that, on the west end of the system, a conventional time freight would make the 133-mile trip from Wyoming to Porter in 5 hours 50 minutes, compared with only 3 hours 26 minutes for the *Overnighter*, only 15 minutes longer than the fastest passenger train timing. These faster times would not survive World War II, which brought longer and heavier trains.

The PM loved its Berkshires and wanted more. In the months before the United States entered the war, the PM bought another twelve locomotives, designating them the N-1 class, numbered 1216–1227, and listed by the manufacturer as order No. 1155. Among the engines was serial number 7839, destined to become No. 1225. The new engines were slightly heavier than the original N-class 2-8-4s, but otherwise were identical. Meanwhile, with another expansion of the 2-8-4 fleet, the railroad lengthened another eight stalls at the Wyoming roundhouse.

Parts of the world already were at war on November 4, 1941, as a gleaming 1225 was pushed out of the Lima plant and into the daylight. Lima's company photographer, Don Jardine, put a sheet of 8-by-10-inch film into his view camera and quickly made a series of photographs of both sides of the locomotive, in keeping with the builder's practice of maintaining thorough visual records of each engine. A few days later, No. 1225 was delivered to the PM at Toledo.

The new machine went straight to work, hauling freight out of the Detroit area. On November 29, photographer Lynn E. Taylor caught up with a still-gleaming 1225 pulling a train through Delray Junction on the southwest side of Detroit. The firebox still sported a set of metal covers over the washout plugs, items a shop crew would dispose of the first time the locomotive went in for regular maintenance. The engineer exuberantly blew the whistle and rang the bell, oblivious to what would happen eight days later.

Nickel Plate 2-8-4 No. 765, the future excursion star, arrives at the yard in Bellevue, Ohio, early on a 1949 morning with a perishables train from Chicago and the West. Photo by Richard J. Cook, courtesy of *Trains* magazine collection.

LAND OF THE BERKSHIRES

The Berkshires helped transform the Pere Marquette (PM) into a competitive front-line railroad, but the PM was not the ultimate showcase for these engines. That status was reserved for the Nickel Plate Road (NKP).

From the moment the Van Sweringen brothers added the NKP to their portfolio, their idea was to turn the railroad into a high-speed bridge route to give bigger railroads such as the New York Central a run for their money for traffic between Buffalo and Chicago and St. Louis. The only way the strategy would work was to develop a locomotive that could offer a near-perfect combination of speed, horsepower, and availability. Because the NKP was a key participant in the Van Sweringens' unified Advisory Mechanical Committee (AMC), the railroad got what it wanted. And then some.

Several railroads fielded Berkshires. The largest fleet belonged to the Erie, which had 105 machines built in 1927 and 1929; they basically were extensions of Lima Locomotive Works' groundbreaking A-1 2-8-4 of 1925. The Chesapeake & Ohio (C&O) had 129 of the AMC's 2-8-4 design, but called them Kanawhas, after a river in West Virginia. Illinois Central operated fifty-one Berkshires. The 2-8-4 was a success everywhere it ran.

But it was on the NKP that the Berkshire achieved true fame. From the first order of fifteen S-class machines from Alco, through a subsequent three orders of S-1, S-2, and S-3 engines from Lima, the NKP's original fleet of eighty 2-8-4s, numbered 700 through 779, were the ideal match for the railroad's basic business model of running relatively short, fast freight trains. NKP historian John A. Rehor put the 700s in perspective: "There are those who assert that the Nickel Plate Berkshire was the most successful steam locomotive ever built for freight service, and their argument is hard to resist. Certainly, no locomotive was more perfectly designed for the job it had to do."[3]

The NKP engines proved their worthiness time and again in the 1930s and through the war years, but it was in their last decade that the reputation became legend. The big Berks kept running off the miles deep into the 1950s, long after the C&O had dumped the fires of the 1200s on its Pere Marquette District. And the longer the 700s ran, the more they attracted a new breed of pioneering railroad photographers who were shaking things up in the pages of *Trains* magazine. They descended en masse on the NKP main line across northern Ohio and Indiana, making some of the most exciting images of the steam era. The Berkshire devotees included Richard J. Cook, Jim Shaughnessy, Philip R. Hastings, Don Wood, and John Rehor.

The 700s had amazing staying power because the locomotives made management happy. In a January 23, 1953, speech to the New York Society of Security Analysts, NKP president Lynne L. White directly confronted the issue of diesel versus steam, acknowledging that the NKP had turned all its passenger service and most of its yard work to diesels. But for the NKP's bread and butter—its high-speed freight service—White still preached the gospel of the Super Power 2-8-4.

> We pride ourselves . . . on supplying "Nickel Plate High Speed Service." Perhaps you've seen it advertised on our cabooses. But it is more than a slogan to decorate the cabooses—it is a promise to our shipper and a challenge to our operating department. We seldom fail to make our connections, and that means fast trains of moderate length instead of tonnage trains built up possibly at the price of not making eastern and western connections. For that service, these engines [the 80 Berkshires] are ideally suited.

For the moment, White said, the railroad was deferring any huge investments in diesels for road-freight service. "We are willing, if necessary, to trade a little bit of added operating expense for added long-haul revenue. . . . Our present steam power is relatively new, is designed for our kind of operation, and therefore there is little difference in operating costs. Indeed, as recently as the summer of 1948 we ran some test of our 'S' engines against both 6,000-h.p. and 4,500-h.p. diesels and you couldn't put *this* piece of paper between the comparative costs."

White's defense of steam was defiant, and the NKP proudly kept running its Berkshires into the space age, right past the October 1957 launch of Russia's *Sputnik*. But in 1958 came the inevitable: the NKP stepped up its purchase of diesels. On July 2, 1958, engine 746 closed out the Berkshire era with a train from Bellevue to Conneaut, Ohio. The railroad kept its 2-8-4s stored and ready for some time to follow, but management's hopes of using them again never bore fruit. Perhaps it's a measure of the NKP's Berk's greatness that a total of six of them survive, mostly in museums and as park engines, along with one very active member of the class, Fort Wayne's 765.

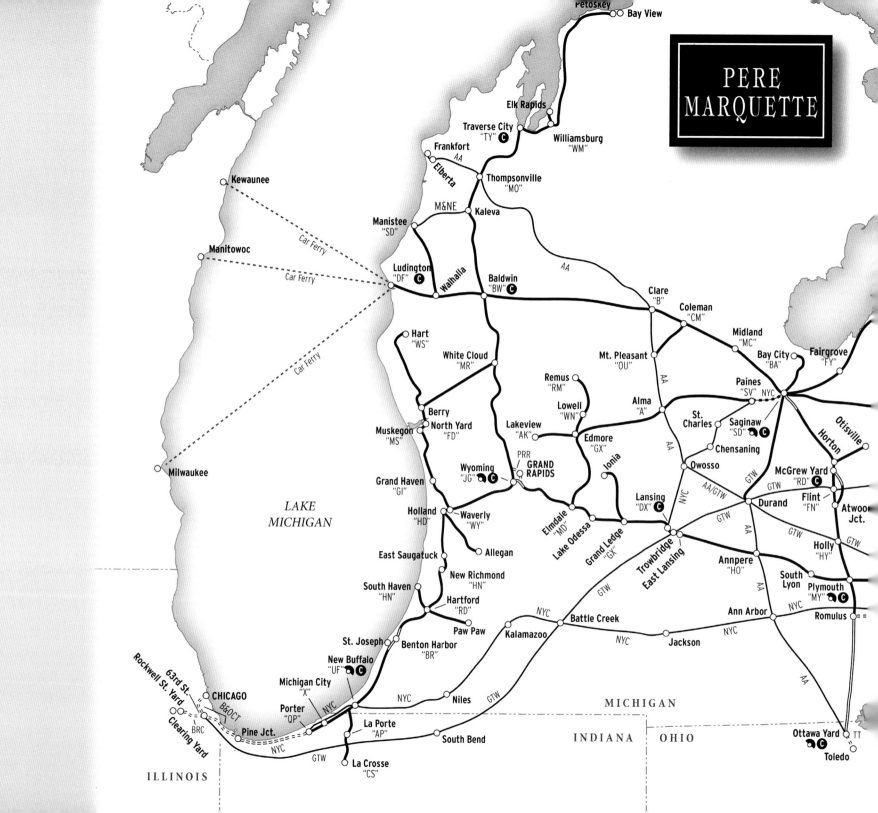

PERE MARQUETTE

Petoskey
Bay View
Elk Rapids
Traverse City "TY" C
Williamsburg "WM"
Frankfort
Elberta
AA
Thompsonville "MO"
M&NE
Kaleva
Manistee "SD"
Ludington "DF" C
Walhalla
Baldwin "BW" C
AA
Clare "B"
Coleman "CM"
Midland "MC"
Bay City "BA"
Fairgrove "FY"
Hart "WS"
White Cloud "MR"
Mt. Pleasant "OU"
AA
Paines "SV"
NYC
Otisville
Remus "RM"
Alma "A"
St. Charles
Saginaw "SD" C
Horton
Berry
North Yard "FD"
Lowell "WN"
AA
Muskegon "MS"
Lakeview "AK"
Edmore "GX"
Chensaning
McGrew Yard "RD" C
PRR
GRAND RAPIDS
Ionia
Owosso
Wyoming "JG" C
Flint "FN"
Atwood Jct.
Grand Haven "GI"
Lansing "DX" C
AA/GTW
Durand
GTW
Holland "HD"
Waverly "WY"
Elmdale "MD"
Lake Odessa
Grand Ledge "GX"
Trowbridge East Lansing
GTW
Annpere "HO"
Holly "HY"
GTW
South Lyon
East Saugatuck
Allegan
GTW
AA
Plymouth "MY" C
New Richmond "HN"
South Haven "HN"
Hartford "RD"
NYC
Battle Creek
Ann Arbor
NYC
Romulus
LAKE MICHIGAN
Paw Paw
Kalamazoo
NYC
Jackson
AA
St. Joseph
Benton Harbor "BR"
New Buffalo "UF" C
Michigan City "X"
NYC
Niles
GTW
MICHIGAN
Kewaunee
Car Ferry
Manitowoc
Car Ferry
Car Ferry
Milwaukee
63rd St.
Rockwell St. Yard
CHICAGO
B&OCT
Porter "QP"
NYC
La Porte "AP"
South Bend
INDIANA OHIO
BRC
Pine Jct.
Clearing Yard
NYC
GTW
La Crosse "CS"
Ottawa Yard C
TT
Toledo
ILLINOIS

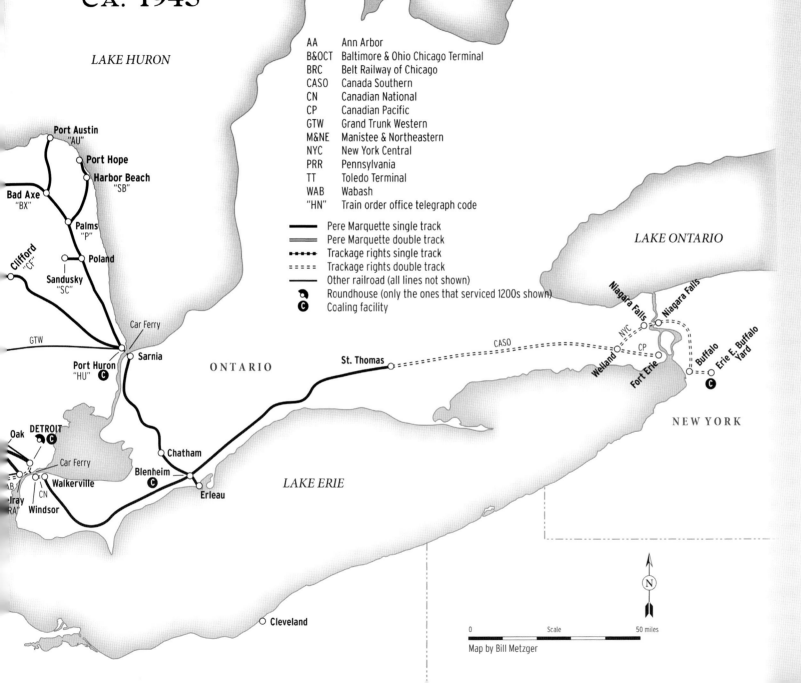

PERE MARQUETTE IN THE BERKSHIRE ERA
CA. 1945

LAKE HURON

LAKE ONTARIO

AA	Ann Arbor
B&OCT	Baltimore & Ohio Chicago Terminal
BRC	Belt Railway of Chicago
CASO	Canada Southern
CN	Canadian National
CP	Canadian Pacific
GTW	Grand Trunk Western
M&NE	Manistee & Northeastern
NYC	New York Central
PRR	Pennsylvania
TT	Toledo Terminal
WAB	Wabash
"HN"	Train order office telegraph code

Pere Marquette single track
Pere Marquette double track
Trackage rights single track
Trackage rights double track
Other railroad (all lines not shown)
Roundhouse (only the ones that serviced 1200s shown)
Coaling facility

Port Austin "AU"
Port Hope
Harbor Beach "SB"
Bad Axe "BX"
Palms "P"
Poland
Clifford "CF"
Sandusky "SC"
Car Ferry
Sarnia
GTW
Port Huron "HU"
ONTARIO
St. Thomas
CASO
Niagara Falls
Niagara Falls
NYC
CP
Welland
Fort Erie
Buffalo
Erie E. Buffalo Yard
NEW YORK
Oak
DETROIT
Car Ferry
Chatham
Blenheim
Walkerville
CN
Erleau
LAKE ERIE
AB
Iray
RA
Windsor

Cleveland

N

0   Scale   50 miles

Map by Bill Metzger

► The Wyoming shops are humming on a wartime footing as crews working in and around the smokebox of a Berkshire perform Class IV repairs in September 1943. Courtesy of C&O Historical Society collection.

CHAPTER 3

BERKSHIRES BECOME WARRIORS

When the Pere Marquette (PM) bought Berkshires from Lima in 1937 and 1941, the purchase culminated the railroad's transformation from a minor player in timber and agriculture into a major heavy-haul railroad. The elite 1200-class locomotives immediately produced dividends, hauling fast freights on tight schedules over a physical plant the railroad could not have imagined twenty years earlier. By going with the Berkshires, PM executives in Cleveland could congratulate themselves for investing in key business assets that, by dint of their efficiency and reliability, would make the company money.

What PM management in Terminal Tower couldn't have foreseen was that their beautiful Berkshires would end up answering a higher calling, hauling the railroad off to war. They'd be expected to do more than even Will Woodard and Lima Locomotive Works had intended. The twelve locomotives of the N-1 class of 1941 arrived just in time for battle. Most of the class had been delivered by the end of November 1941, just days before the Japanese attack on Pearl Harbor.

The American railroad industry and its employees would prove to be as critical to the Allied victory as the soldiers, pilots, sailors, bombers, ships, and tanks thrown directly into harm's way. Battered by the Depression, many of them emerging from bankruptcy, U.S. railroads performed

I̶N̲ ̲T̲H̲E̲ "battle of production" the railroads of America are becoming increasingly important—and this applies with full force to Pere Marquette. When tanks, planes and guns swing into action on some distant battle-field, the shipping tags will long since have been discarded. But vital parts of every important battle are the original routing orders—often reading "Via Pere Marquette"—starting these fighting tools on their long journeys to the battle fronts. ★ Pere Marquette is on the offensive. Our product is transportation—and, twenty-four hours every day, our plant and personnel are producing more and more of it—in the name of *Freedom!*

PERE MARQUETTE
Railway

THE RAILROAD THAT CROSSES LAKE MICHIGAN

May 23, 1942

39

LIMA-BUILT
2-8-4 STEAM LOCOMOTIVES

speed PERE MARQUETTE traffic

T̲O̲ meet steadily increasing demands for more rapid movement of heavy freight traffic, Pere Marquette has continued to add to its fleet of Lima-built 2-8-4s, so that today thirty-nine of these modern steam locomotives are speeding the freight service on its lines.

LIMA LOCOMOTIVE WORKS INCORPORATED, LIMA, OHIO

May 11, 1946

31

heroically, including the resurgent PM. David P. Morgan, the dean of railroad journalists, characterized it this way: "Railroading's finest hour lasted 45 months and produced the finest testimony of all time for the efficiency of the flanged wheel on the steel rail."[1]

The statistics are amazing. Over the course of World War II, railroads hauled more than 90 percent of all military hardware and 97 percent of all troops. The industry nearly doubled its ton-mile output and quadrupled its passenger traffic. Revenue ton-miles, a basic measurement of freight-hauling productivity, grew from 373.3 billion in 1940 to 740 billion in 1944. At the height of the war, approximately 2,500 special troop trains operated every month. In one year, 1943, the railroads took 10 million troops off to service.

Located in one of the nation's strategic industrial regions, the PM was ready for the war effort. Years of investment had yielded a railroad with a first-class physical plant, boasting main lines with 110- and 112-pound rail, rock ballast, automatic block signals, and the growing use of centralized traffic control. Now, with twenty-seven new Berkshires, it had locomotives to match.

The investment paid off after the War Production Board's decision in January 1942 to cease the manufacturing of civilian cars and trucks. Auto plants across Michigan shifted to a war footing, with the PM shouldering its share of the output. Ford built B24 Liberator bombers for the Army Air Corps at its new Willow Run plant near Ypsilanti and aircraft engines for Pratt & Whitney at the River Rouge plant, adjacent to the PM's huge Rougemere yard. Chrysler made anti-aircraft guns and military tugboats at plants in Detroit and M3 and M4 tanks at a new plant in Warren. General Motors (GM) converted to making the M4 tank at the Fisher Body plants in Flint and Grand Blanc, ammunition casings at Buick plants, and forgings for tanks and military trucks at Oldsmobile in Lansing. In Toledo, the Willys plant stepped up production of its famous Jeep, with additional production of the redoubtable vehicle moving to Ford.

In addition to hauling much of the finished war materiel, the PM became a vital artery for delivering the raw materials for all those factories. The key commodity was coal from its sister carrier, the Chesapeake & Ohio (C&O), via the Toledo gateway. By 1943, the PM was

◄◄ The Pere Marquette declared its dedication to the war effort in this ad from the May 23, 1942, edition of the trade magazine *Railway Age*. Courtesy of *Trains* magazine collection.

◄ In 1944, the Pere Marquette beefed up its motive-power roster with eleven additional 2-8-4s in the N-2 class, as promoted in this ad from Lima. Courtesy of *Trains* magazine collection.

annually handling more than 198,000 loaded cars arriving from all its connections, and the C&O accounted for 73,000 of those loads, mostly coal.

The Berkshires were in the thick of the battle. Operations out of Wyoming in 1943 illustrate how hard the engines worked. A report from January of that year showed that the 2-8-4s ran 48,504 revenue miles on the Chicago Division alone. The average day's work for an engine was 229 miles, which was excellent considering the servicing demands of the typical large steam locomotive, and far better than the PM's old 2-8-2s or 2-10-2s could provide.

Sometimes even excellent wasn't good enough, not at first. Early in the war, PM general manager M. M. "Mike" Cronk decided the railroad wasn't hustling enough, and in a memo exhorted his superintendents, "During January, our serviceable road engines made an average . . . of 126 miles a day, but the figure for the year 1942 is lower than that of 1941. I cannot over-emphasize the importance that must be attached to this matter. . . . The faster we turn our power at Chicago, New Buffalo and Detroit in the direction of Wyoming, the greater mileage we will find our heavier power making."[2]

Cronk's frustration notwithstanding, the PM embraced its wartime responsibilities and, like all U.S. railroads of the era, was eager to say so. One PM ad in May 1942 showed an army tank, a staple of the railroad's wartime traffic base, with the stenciled headline "VIA PM RWY." The ad copy proclaimed, "Our product is transportation—and twenty-four hours every day, our plant and personnel are producing more and more of it—in the name of Freedom!"

◆　　◆　　◆

As gallant as the first 1200s were, the PM needed reinforcements. The tide of war traffic proved to be too much for just the original twenty-seven Berkshires, so in April 1943 the railroad made a third and final order for another eleven, classifying them as N-2 and numbered 1228–1239. Because Lima was also making tanks, the builder could not deliver the new engines until February and March 1944, but the N-2s nonetheless brought the PM important new horsepower.

▶ Pere Marquette 2-8-4 1228 accelerates upgrade with a westbound freight near Benton Harbor, Michigan, in 1950. Photo by Merwyn Chapin, courtesy of *Trains* magazine collection.

The new N-2 engines boasted improvements over the original N and N-1 Berkshires. A significant new feature was the use of all cast-steel frames, instead of the "built-up," bolted frames on the earlier 2-8-4s. The N-2s also cut a slightly different profile: the steam dome was placed behind the sand box, as was common practice on the C&O. The N-2s were heavier, too, and like the previous N-1 class, the last five (1235–1239) were equipped with boosters.

Throughout the war, the railroad continued to get great service out of its 2-8-4s. The engines were efficient, going farther than any of the older engines on a tender full of water. They could make the 114-mile Wyoming-to-New Buffalo run, for instance, on a single tank. The most consistent problems reported were minor: a tendency for foaming of the water in the boiler, perhaps the result of the PM's methods of water treatment, and depressed performance because of poor coal, which showed up more often during the war years.

Nowhere was the wartime show on the PM more spectacular than at a place called New Richmond hill, a 2-mile section of

► Berkshire 1220 reaches the top of the New Richmond grade at East Saugatuck. Visible just to the left of the locomotive, in the far distance, is the exhaust plume of a helper engine pushing on the rear of the train. Photo by Richard Pedler, courtesy of *Trains* magazine collection.

1.23-percent grade south of Holland where the main line descended from flat farm country into the Kalamazoo River valley. The track approached the river from both sides via a series of S-curves and crossed on a single-track deck bridge at the picturesque hamlet of New Richmond.

Throughout their service on the PM, the normally self-reliant 1200s were obliged to pick up helper locomotives for most trains either at a siding called East Saugatuck on the north end of the hill or at New Richmond on the south. The helpers were based out of Waverly Yard in Holland, and mostly were either 2-8-2s or 2-10-2s. In later years, a Berkshire occasionally was known to lend a sister engine a hand. Whatever the pairing, New Richmond hill constantly shook with the thunder of doubleheaded PM steam.

◆　◆　◆

Even as the 2-8-4s put on their muscular show, the PM's mechanical department was getting its toe in the water with a new form of motive power, the diesel-electric. The revolution had begun quietly in June 1939 with the arrival in Wyoming of SW1 switcher No. 10, a small,

▲ Pere Marquette's first diesel locomotive, SW1 No. 10, shuffles freight cars along the Detroit River beneath the Ambassador Bridge. Courtesy of *Trains* magazine collection.

▶ The twilight of Pere Marquette steam: renumbered and relettered for new owner Chesapeake & Ohio, No. 2695 races through Grandville, Michigan, with a westbound train in November 1949. The locomotive displays raised number boards, characteristic of C&O engines. Photo by Frank A. Anthony, courtesy of *Trains* magazine collection.

600-horsepower locomotive built by the Electro-Motive Corporation (EMC) of La Grange, Illinois, a southwest suburb of Chicago. Already a subsidiary of GM, EMC was making waves with its trailblazing E-series passenger diesels, introduced in 1937, and its FT freight diesels, which debuted in 1939. The PM's unit was powered by an early version of EMC's soon-to-be famous 2-stroke, 6-cylinder 567-model engine, the power plant that would revolutionize railroading after the war.

The little switcher was unpretentious, painted black, and lettered like the steam locomotives. It was put to work in yards in Detroit and Port Huron, and later in local freight service around the Thumb. The railroad bought a second SW1, numbered 11, in 1942, and placed it in similar service. War Production Board restrictions soon went into place, postponing the development of further diesel-electrics, but not before the PM ordered four more diesels from EMC, this time a quartet of 1,000-horsepower NW2 units, also for switching.

◆　◆　◆

With the end of the war in August 1945, America's railroads confronted business realities that had been interrupted in 1941. One of them was the slow but certain movement toward consolidation. For the PM, that meant the inevitable deepening of ties to the C&O. The C&O was commonly called "Chessie," a name also adopted for the kitten icon used to promote its passenger trains, and had emerged from the war in strong condition, thanks to the riches that poured from Virginia's and West Virginia's coal mines.

The C&O's special interest in the PM traced back to 1931, when the Alleghany Corporation's indebtedness forced the Van Sweringen brothers to sell some of their holdings. Rather than sell to outsiders, Alleghany "drafted" the C&O—still solvent, still paying dividends—to obtain Alleghany's holdings of 42,000 shares of PM stock. In fact, the transaction wasn't in cash. In effect, the Van Sweringens traded the C&O's good credit for Alleghany's bad, with the PM as a pawn. This gave the C&O practical control of its Michigan cousin.

The war kept the original Van Sweringen companies in place for another few years, but the postwar era brought the beginning of a movement toward large mergers, with the PM and the C&O in the vanguard. The two railroads had coordinated closely throughout the war. Now, the larger C&O was free to claim the traffic and revenue opportunities obvious in a classic end-to-end merger.

The PM's attractions were made clear in January 1945, when David A. Hill, a railroad securities consultant in Chicago, made a four-day inspection trip of the PM aboard a special train of business cars. He concluded that the PM had a positive outlook for traffic and earnings based on its automotive traffic and the growth of the bridge traffic over the Niagara frontier. The latter, he noted, had grown from 14.4 percent of all PM traffic in 1937 to 29.8 percent by 1943.

Hill admired the PM's tidy operations, but he also could see where all this was going, and he couldn't resist invoking the C&O's popular symbol. "The Kitten is now grown up and does not need help from Chessie. Institutions do not need to lean on C&O in buying Pere Marquette bonds," he wrote. "Be that as it may, I feel that after Chessie sees what a nice kitten Pere Marquette has become, she will eventually take him home and admit of the parentage."

Pere Marquette 1225 hustles a westbound freight train along the Union Belt Railroad at Solvay Street in Detroit in August 1944. Photo by Ernest L. Novak photo, courtesy of *Trains* magazine collection.

The inevitable became official two years later when the PM merged with the C&O on June 6, 1947, in what was virtually an outright acquisition. The price for the PM was $114,227,199. The entire Michigan-based railroad instantly became the C&O's "Pere Marquette District."

In giving its blessing to the union, the Interstate Commerce Commission (ICC) noted the interlocking Van Sweringen management that dated from 1929: "Under this joint management both carriers have profited in economies and increased traffic." The merger "would not lessen competition, but would create a strong, well-balanced system that would afford stiffer competition to the [New York Central], [Pennsylvania], [Baltimore & Ohio] and other railroads," the ICC concluded.

◆   ◆   ◆

Although the C&O would manage the PM as an autonomous property for several years, it dramatically changed the operational landscape by moving fast on dieselization. With War Production Board restrictions gone, all U.S. railroads could get back to where they

left off with internal combustion. On the PM, the relative newness of the Berkshire fleet would have little effect.

But before the C&O could get rid of PM steam, the railroad decided to renumber all the 1200-class 2-8-4s. This was done ostensibly to integrate the PM engines into the C&O's own fleet of 129 2-8-4 Kanawhas, which were a mainstay in coal country. The C&O worked out a new numbering schedule for the PM engines that renumbered class N 1201–1215 to C&O N-3 2685–2699, class N-1 1216–1227

▲ Symbol of transition: already lettered for the Chesapeake & Ohio, an ungainly BL2 "branch line" unit is ready for delivery to the C&O's Pere Marquette District in February 1949. Courtesy of *Trains* magazine collection.

◄ Using the Pere Marquette's trackage rights on the New York Central, 1227 races past steel mills in Gary, Indiana, with an eastbound freight train. Photo by Br. Andrew Corsini, courtesy of *Trains* magazine collection.

to C&O N-1 2650–2661, and class N-2 1228–1239 to C&O N-2 2670–2681. However, equipment trust agreements required that the locomotives remain lettered for the PM until the trusts expired, and only the first fifteen engines actually got their new numbers. The 1225 stayed the 1225, and so on.

Meanwhile, the railroad pushed ahead on the diesel front. Although the PM had stood pat on diesels after 1942, as soon as the war ended in August 1945 the railroad plunged back into acquiring power from what was now the Electro-Motive Division (EMD) of GM. First came ten more NW2s in 1945, and then, in September 1946, an order for six 1,500-horsepower BL2s, so designated for "branch-line" service. Although the BL2s were not delivered until mid-1948, a year after the C&O's acquisition of the PM, the BL2s nonetheless showed the railroad what slightly bigger diesels could do. After the merger, the new PM District of the C&O acquired eight more.

The BL2 turned out to be an oddity among diesels, but for a time the PM was its showcase. The locomotive actually was

► The conquerors: doing the work of what was formerly a single 2-8-4, a pair of GP7 diesels depart Plymouth with a Toledo-bound freight in the early 1950s. Photo by Robert A. Hadley, courtesy of *Trains* magazine collection.

▲ The railroad gained national attention with the introduction of its *Pere Marquette* streamliner, hauled by an E7 diesel, shown here departing Detroit's Fort Street Union Depot for Grand Rapids in May 1948. Photo by Elmer Treloar, courtesy of *Trains* magazine collection.

▶ With 2-8-4 No. 1227 leading 2-8-2 No. 1067, double-headed Pere Marquette steam leads an eastbound train toward the Kalamazoo River at the bottom of New Richmond hill. Photo by Richard Pedler, courtesy of *Trains* magazine collection.

a hybrid of EMD's successful cab-unit and switcher designs, and as such was of limited capability. Streamlined but ungainly, the BL2 offered limited rearward visibility and unsatisfactory on-and-off access for a brakeman. But the experience with them in Michigan was encouraging enough to cause the C&O to go big on the next major product from EMD, the GP7, the first widely successful general-purpose hood unit. Using its PM District as a proving ground, the C&O received twenty GP7s from EMD in 1950, nineteen more in early 1951 from EMD's GM subsidiary in Canada (for use on the Canadian lines), and a huge order of fifty-nine in late 1951 and early 1952. The ruthlessly efficient Geeps, as they were known, quickly shouldered aside the Berkshires.

The PM also made a splash with diesels in passenger service in 1946 by introducing the *Pere Marquette* streamliners, a fleet of passenger trains operating in day service between Detroit, Lansing, and Grand Rapids. The *Pere Marquettes* featured coach, parlor, and dining service in stainless steel cars built by Pullman-Standard, but it was the power up front that attracted the most attention: sleek Electro-Motive E7 diesels, the basic design of which became the standard passenger locomotive for a generation.

Across the board, in freight and passenger service, the new diesels performed well, and C&O management decided to dieselize all operations on the PM by the end of 1951. First to drop steam was the Canadian District by the end of 1950, then, in order, the Saginaw and Grand Rapids Districts in 1951. Eleven of the Berkshires received a reprieve when, in March 1951, a surge in coal traffic led the C&O to transfer five to the Chesapeake District, followed by six more. Transferred engines included N-3s 2693–2698, plus N-1s 1218, 1222, and 1226, and N-2s 1230 and 1235. All were retired by April 1953 after working out of Columbus, Ohio; Russell, Kentucky; and Clifton Forge, Virginia.

Back in Michigan, the last active terminal for the PM 2-8-4s was Waverly Yard in Holland, where the final engines were used in helper service over New Richmond hill. The last 2-8-4, alas unidentified, was dispatched on November 25, 1951, from Waverly to Grand

A member of the last class of N-2 Berkshires, Pere Marquette 1229 clatters over the Grand Trunk Western junction at Trowbridge, in East Lansing, with an eastbound freight in June 1950. Photo by James R. Stiefel, courtesy of *Trains* magazine collection.

Rapids to be decommissioned, closing out steam on the PM.[3]

Hundreds of PM railroaders had worked on the gallant Berkshires since 1937, and loved and respected the engines. The 2-8-4s had as profound an effect on the company's fortunes as any motive power on any railroad. But, at the end of the day, the locomotives were business assets, and after 1951 they held value only as scrap metal.

The C&O began selling the 2-8-4s to scrappers beginning in 1954, but thirteen evaded the torch for a time, stored at the old PM freight yard in the little beach town of New Buffalo, in the southwest corner of the state. The equipment trust agreements that originally financed their purchase would not expire until 1958. It was only a temporary stay of execution, and all were sold for scrap by 1961. But not before two engines were pulled from the dead line: they carried the numbers 1223 and 1225.

REPRIEVE IN COAL COUNTRY

No matter how earnest railroads were in their efforts to retire steam locomotives in the 1950s, vagaries of the freight businesses often derailed the scrapping plans, and occasional surges in the traffic brought strange locomotives to strange places. The most famous example came in 1956, when the Pennsylvania Railroad leased eleven of the Santa Fe's magnificent 5000-class 2-10-4s to help the Pennsylvania's own engines handle a crush of freight in Ohio. A similar necessity led the Chesapeake & Ohio (C&O) to lease eleven 4-8-4s from the Richmond, Fredericksburg & Potomac.

A handful of Pere Marquette (PM) Berkshires won a similar reprieve when business on the C&O's main lines in Ohio, West Virginia, and Virginia stretched the railroad's locomotive roster uncomfortably thin. In March 1951, the C&O transferred five PM 2-8-4s to the Chesapeake District, mostly running out of terminals in Columbus, Ohio, and Russell, Kentucky, as well as Clifton Forge, Virginia. Their assignment was to haul

anything the C&O threw at them, but for the most part they handled coal trains.

The first to head south were N-3s 2694–2698, which were free from trust-financing restrictions and already had been renumbered as C&O engines. In April 1952, another six were sent southward, N-1s 1218, 1222, and 1226; N-2s 1230 and 1235; and N-3 2693, all still carrying their PM numbers and inscription, as required by the trust agreements. All these engines presumably were chosen because they were in the best mechanical condition.

However they were numbered or painted, the PM engines cut a different figure in traditional C&O territory, where the railroad's Kanawha 2-8-4s held sway. With their centered headlights and traditional boiler-tube pilots, the PM engines looked more elegant than the utilitarian Kanawhas they were there to supplement. Engine crews were happy to get the new engines because the PM's maintenance was known to be more meticulous than the C&O's. The Michigan engines simply ran well.

In their book *Pere Marquette Power*, authors Art Million and Thomas Dixon cited a recollection by Roy B. Anderson, a machinist at Clifton Forge. "It was almost like the excitement in the gone times when new power arrived," wrote Anderson. "This was particularly true because everyone recognized them as no ordinary steam engine or hand-me-down. The 2696 was one of the last locomotives to go through the backshop here in 1952, and it was very apparent to all the old mechanics that this 15-year-old steamer had been maintained far beyond the standards of the C&O's over the same period."

In a sad irony, the eleven PM engines sent to coal country were the last to operate but also the first to be scrapped. While a large group of Berkshires stored up in Michigan lingered into the late 1950s at New Buffalo, the engines transferred to the C&O were cut up either in 1952 or 1953, after only a few months of service. Beautifully maintained they may have been, but that wasn't enough to hold back the C&O's surging Geeps.

Ex–Pere Marquette 2-8-4 No. 2695 hauls loaded coal hopper cars westbound over the Jefferson River bridge on the Chesapeake & Ohio's James River Line, near Clifton Forge, Virginia, in November 1952. Photo by G. David Graeff, courtesy of *Trains* magazine collection.

On March 28, 1961, nearly four years after 1225's installment at Michigan State University, five Pere Marquette 2-8-4s await scrapping at the M. S. Kaplan yard in Gary, Indiana. The locomotives are, in order, 1224, 1229, 1236, 1233, and 1237. Photo by Jim Farrell, courtesy of *Trains* magazine collection.

CHAPTER 4

A LUCKY NUMBER

The steam era on the Chesapeake & Ohio's (C&O's) Pere Marquette District was over by the end of 1951. The ascent of the diesel already had caused the railroad to pick up the pace of retiring and scrapping older, smaller steam locomotives, so the 4-6-2s, 2-8-2s, and 2-10-2s that had formed the backbone of the pre-Berkshire era were the first to go. But it was a certainty the 2-8-4s would quickly follow. The C&O executives in Terminal Tower in Cleveland couldn't afford to be nostalgic, even for perfectly good locomotives that, in some cases, were less than a decade old.

The machinations of the C&O didn't mean much in the college town of East Lansing, home of Michigan State College (MSC). Already a large institution, with 16,000 students in 1951, MSC actually was a minor customer of the C&O, which provided switching service over a mile-long spur to the college's coal-fire power plant along the Red Cedar River, on the north side of Shaw Lane, the main east-west thoroughfare through the campus. An earlier power plant on the north side of the river was served via a railroad bridge.

If the C&O was known to the college community at all, it was probably for the railroad's sleek *Pere Marquette* passenger trains that every weekend carried students home to Grand Rapids or the Detroit area from the railroad's stolid stone depot in downtown Lansing. Other than that, the biggest noise the railroad made at MSC was the sound of its freight trains clattering over

Its white-lined number designating it as surplus, a neglected 1225 is parked adjacent to the coaling tower at Wyoming shops, awaiting restoration as a campus display. Courtesy of B. Bluehamp collection.

the junction at Trowbridge, just west of the campus, where the C&O's trains crossed the Grand Trunk Western's Chicago–Port Huron double-track main line at grade.

MSC was making plenty of its own noise in the postwar years. It was in the early stages of the Hannah Era, named for John Hannah, who became president of the college in 1941. Over the ensuing three decades he would preside over explosive growth at the institution, often seemingly through sheer force of will. In that first year of his presidency MSC boasted an enrollment of approximately 6,000 students. When Hannah retired as a legend in 1969, the student body numbered 39,000.

Hannah was born in 1902 in Grand Rapids to a family intensely interested in horticulture but also (and especially) chickens. After graduating from Grand Rapids Junior College, he enrolled in the University of Michigan's law school. But Hannah later decided the law wasn't for him, and he surprised some family and friends by transferring to MSC to get a bachelor's degree in agriculture, specializing in poultry.

John Hannah: as president, he led Michigan State University's astonishing growth through the 1960s.
Courtesy of Michigan State University Archives and Historical Collections.

Hannah started his new career as a very successful extension agent at MSC before taking a post in the Roosevelt administration's National Recovery Administration. But soon he was wooed back to East Lansing to become secretary of both MSC and the State Board of Agriculture, which governed the college. One of Hannah's fellow board members was Forest H. Akers, a Chrysler sales executive with a passion for golf.

When Hannah became president in 1941, he succeeded another legend, Robert S. Shaw, who had led MSC since 1928. In his thirteen-year tenure, Shaw had made substantial progress in moving the former Michigan Agricultural College beyond its farming roots. He was an adept fund-raiser, attracting gifts to the college from a variety of individuals, foundations, and special-interest organizations. He also transformed the institution's administration, hiring a number of professors with impressive academic backgrounds. Shaw's relationship with his most important protégé, John Hannah, took a personal turn in 1938 when his daughter, Sarah, married the ambitious former poultry man.

As the new president, Hannah worked vigorously during his tenure to upgrade MSC's academic standing, but it was inevitable he'd become best known for the historic and even breathtaking physical expansion of the compact MSC campus. Over the decades he would oversee the acquisition of 7,000 acres, and raise tens of millions of dollars—much of them federal—to embark on a massive building campaign. Sprawling dormitories and classroom buildings rose up from the farmland south of the Red Cedar River, which historically marked the southern border of the campus. The new campus spread out across a parklike expanse of boulevards and trees. All of it was meticulously groomed.

The era reached its symbolic peak in 1955, MSC's centennial year, with the Michigan legislature's decision to change the name of the institution to Michigan State University (MSU), a move the University of Michigan Board of Regents had fought for months but eventually lost 23-2 in the state senate.

◆   ◆   ◆

Each year seemed to bring momentous change to the new MSU, no less so in 1957. The university's sprawling new library on West Circle Drive was in its first year of service. Student enrollment hit 26,500, with no signs of slowing down. The football Spartans went 8-1 that year, finishing as the nation's number three team. As if to sanctify that status, Macklin Field, the school's traditional football venue on the south bank of the Red Cedar, was enlarged with top decks to a capacity of 76,000 and renamed Spartan Stadium.

Almost in the shadow of the stadium, the university had built a short two-lane street called Stadium Road, linking Shaw Lane with the southwest corner of the campus. There wasn't much there in 1957, just some practice fields, scattered postwar Quonset huts, and otherwise empty land out to the campus's western perimeter at Harrison Road. Stadium Road was a distant corner of MSU, its most distinguishing feature the railroad spur that ran parallel to the street before it crossed Shaw Lane to reach the university's two power plants. If you were looking for an out-of-way place on the MSU campus, this little stretch of two-lane would do just fine.

◆　　◆　　◆

Forest H. Akers: the Michigan State University benefactor thought the university should preserve 1225. Courtesy of Michigan State University Archives and Historical Collections.

By 1957, the "College Spur" (as the railroad always called it) hosted only C&O diesel switchers and a small, university-owned 44-ton GE locomotive to switch coal cars. Steam whistles had given way to air horns. But even though six years had passed since the last Pere Marquette (PM) steam locomotive dropped its fire, the Pere Marquette District of the C&O still carried those thirteen stored Berkshires on the books.

They were a forlorn collection of engines, sitting out their last days in the unfortunate weather of the West Michigan lakeshore, where the snows can pile up to the tune of 70 inches a year. Among the orphaned locomotives was an unremarked member of the class: 1225. Scarred with lesions of rust, the number on its cab crossed out with an emphatic white line, the onetime Super Power engine simply waited for its turn to be sent to Purdy Company, Hyman-Michaels, or one of the other prominent scrap companies in the Chicago area.

Enter Forest Akers, the automobile executive who served for eighteen years on the State Board of Agriculture, which had given way to the new university's Board of Trustees in 1955. Born in 1886, Akers grew up on a farm near Williamston, a few miles east of East Lansing. As a boy, surely he'd heard the melodious whistles of PM locomotives roaring through town.

Akers attended Michigan Agricultural College from 1905 to 1908, where he had the distinction of playing great baseball and being a troublemaker. He was kicked out after his junior year, partly for poor grades, partly for his shenanigans. But he loved his would-be alma mater, which prompted him to seek the Republican nomination to the agriculture board when, as he said, "nobody else wanted it."

Akers had a great career in the automobile industry. He started out at the REO Motor Car Company in Lansing and moved up steadily through the sales ranks before going over to Dodge in Detroit, where he ultimately became a Chrysler vice president. Over the years he gave a substantial amount of money to MSC and MSU for scholarships. Akers might be best known to today's students for Akers Hall, built in 1964 on the east edge of campus. But his most famous donation is the gift of 300 acres on the south edge of the campus that in 1958 became Forest Akers Golf Course. Today, the two eighteen-hole courses are considered among the best public courses in Michigan.

Forest Akers also had a soft spot for those trains he'd witnessed as a boy in Williamston, a trait that surfaced one day when he was playing golf with Cyrus S. Eaton, chairman of the C&O. That they were golf partners made perfect sense. Chrysler was an important C&O customer, with assembly plants and affiliated suppliers located across the railroad's northern territory. Somehow the conversation turned to the steam locomotives the C&O was cutting up. Eaton had a romantic streak in him and suggested that scrapping all of them would be a shame. Couldn't one of the engines be preserved at the university?

While there is no formal record of their conversation, Akers apparently thought "yes." With that gentlemen's agreement on the links, coupled with Akers's confidence that he could get his

Cyrus S. Eaton: the Chesapeake & Ohio chairman was eager to save another steam locomotive. *Courtesy of Trains magazine collection.*

old friend John Hannah to accept it, one of the engines down in New Buffalo won salvation from the acetylene torch.

But which one?

It's unclear why 1225 turned out to be the lucky number. One prevalent story holds that someone attached the numbers to Christmas: December 25, or 1225. Another is that 1225 appeared to be in better shape than the other 2-8-4s parked nearby. This is doubtful. The C&O had dramatically reduced maintenance on the 1200s in the last couple of years, and all of the Berkshires had been run hard. Records indicate that 1225's last major shopping at Wyoming had come in 1950, when the main cylinders were rebored, but not much else was done. Presumably the engine got very little maintenance in its last months, and its firebox and working parts were worn. Probably the best of the 1200s were sent south to the C&O.

What most likely happened in New Buffalo was that 1225 was the easiest to remove. It's possible the engine was the last one backed into storage, and hence could be towed away with a minimum of switching. Whatever criteria prevailed, the locomotive was transported to the Wyoming shops in early 1957 and parked for a time adjacent to the huge coaling tower that serviced the engine so many years earlier. Eventually, workers at Wyoming gave 1225 a serviceable, cosmetic restoration. (Three years later, 1225's only surviving sister, 1223, also would escape the scrap line at New Buffalo. After a fund-raising effort by Detroit schoolchildren, 1223 was selected for display at the Michigan State Fairgrounds in Detroit.)

◆ ◆ ◆

Only an MSU supporter with the clout of an Akers could have foisted a steam locomotive on the university. There does not appear to be any record of Akers's communication with John Hannah, but at some point the benefactor informed the president of his "gift," and things were dutifully set in motion. Hannah's true feelings were apparent later when he wrote that "the university should get it, park it somewhere and put a sign on it, giving it minimum maintenance over the years."[1]

Meanwhile, someone at MSU had to own the locomotive. Akers had suggested the College of Engineering. But the college's dean, John D. Ryder, didn't want it. This was, after all, 1957, the International Geophysical Year, a worldwide event celebrating the ascendancy of new science and technology. MSU was mindful of it. In that context, there was no place for an old steam locomotive. In an interview years later, Ryder was dismissive of 1225 and said so in terms any engineer would understand. "Here was a machine (1225) designed to work up to tolerances of 1,000th of an inch. We're already dealing with things at a millionth of an inch," he scoffed.[2]

And so the default for 1225 became the MSU Museum, a venerable campus institution known for its stuffed birds and animals. The responsibility for caring for it fell to museum director Rollin H. Baker, who headed the institution from 1955 to 1982. It would be fair to say that the museum, with its orientation toward natural history and anthropology, was an even less appropriate choice than the College of Engineering.

The museum traces its history to 1857

By the time 1225 was being refurbished by Wyoming for Michigan State University, the stalls of the old roundhouse were populated by the GP7 diesels that put steam out of business. Courtesy of Trains magazine collection.

and occupied various facilities over the years. For a time it was on the third floor of the 1925 library, but in 1940 the museum moved to the ground floor of the new Auditorium, a large performing arts facility on Farm Lane, one of a number of new structures financed in part by the Public Works Administration. In 1956, the university built a new library on West Circle Drive, across the river from the stadium. At the time it was the fifth-largest university library building in the United States. As a consequence, an expanded MSU Museum moved back into the vacated 1925 library, where it remains today.

In 1957, the museum's mission had little to do with mechanical history, let alone locomotives or railroads. The largest single category of exhibits was zoological; for many years the museum curator had been a member of the zoology department. A favorite attraction for generations of schoolchildren was a floor of habitat dioramas featuring elk, hawk, bison, and other examples of the taxidermist's art. The museum had an amazing variety of other exhibits, too, reflecting the unpredictable, even crazy predilections of benefactors and alumni: a large collection of firearms showing the development of modern weaponry, including a sixteenth-century English crossbow; a Bolivian mummy donated by the U.S. ambassador to Bolivia; woven Native American baskets donated by Gladys Olds Anderson of Lansing. And, suddenly in 1957, a 220-ton steam locomotive.

Before 1225 was delivered from Wyoming, the C&O instructed shop forces to change the lettering on the locomotive's sandbox and tender from PERE MARQUETTE to CHESAPEAKE & OHIO. The engine was towed to East Lansing, moved onto the MSU spur at Trowbridge, and parked on a short section of track along Stadium Road, facing north. The trip from Wyoming wasn't without incident: at some point the babbitt metal friction bearing on the engineer's side of the front wheelset, called the pony truck, began to seriously overheat to the point it was ruined. But what would that matter? The engine wasn't going to run again.

After installing the locomotive, crews disconnected the display track from the power-plant spur. This simple move carried some meaning, physically isolating 1225 from the rest of the U.S. rail system.

▶ A small audience and a handful of dignitaries gathered on Stadium Road for the June 10, 1957, dedication of 1225. Courtesy of Michigan State University Archives and Historical Collections.

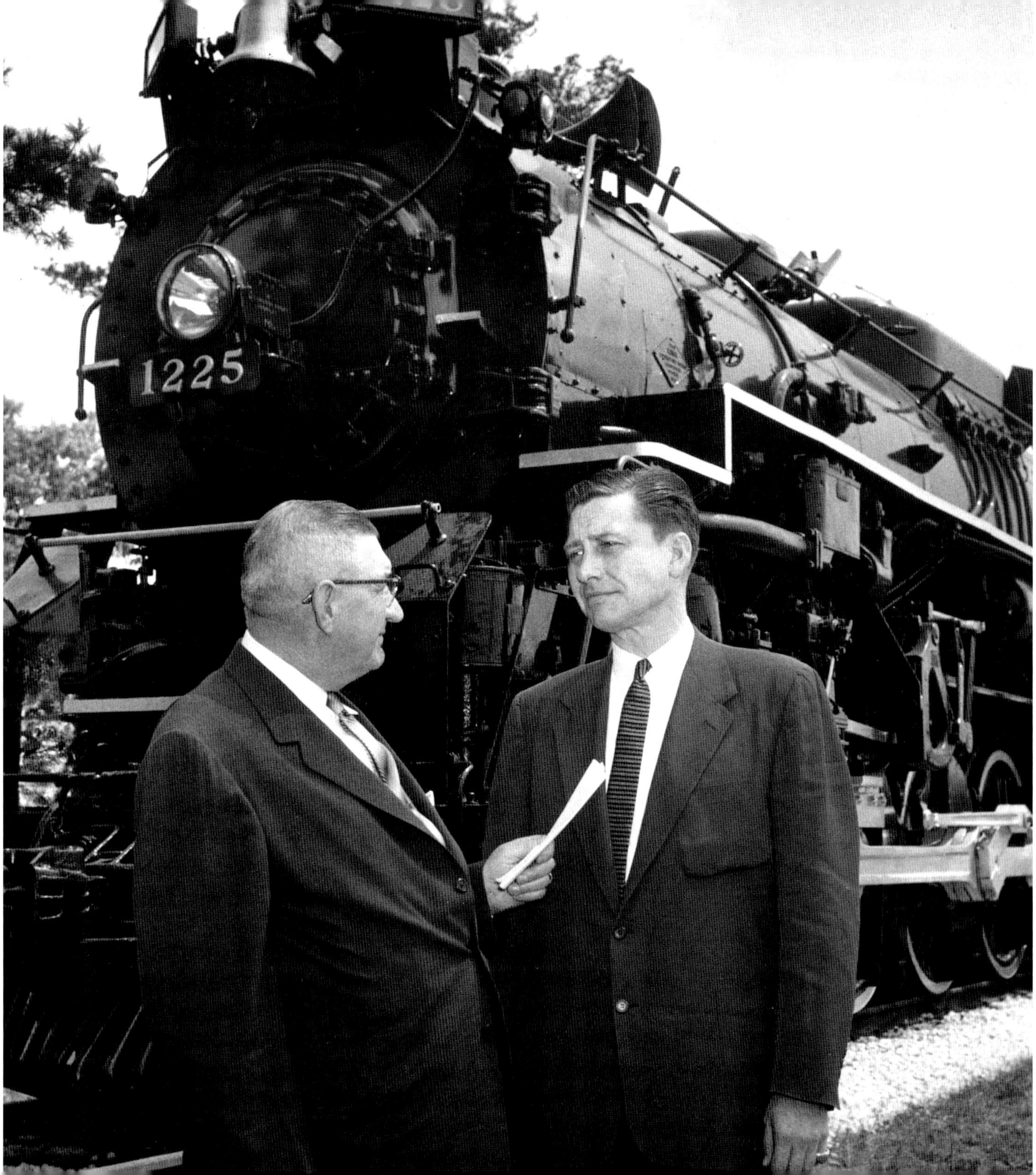
1225

Gleaming in fresh black paint, 1225 was dedicated at a special ceremony on June 10, 1957. It was a brilliantly sunny day in the high 70s. A simple portable stage was erected beside the engine's firebox, with a podium and chairs for five dignitaries, facing a small audience sitting in folding chairs set up on the pavement.

Representing the university was Vice President Thomas Hamilton, who, judging from his weak smile in photographs taken that day, would have preferred to be elsewhere. In 1959, Hamilton would leave MSU to become chancellor of the State University of New York system, and later he became president of the University of Hawaii. Representing the C&O was a bemused C. J. Milliken, the railroad's general manager of the Northern Region. Although there is no record of all the attendees, it's nearly a certainty that John Hannah did not show up.

If the reporting on 1225's arrival by the *Michigan State News* is any indication, even the university's daily paper knew how Hannah felt about his new acquisition. There was no story on the locomotive on either the day of the dedication or the day after. Finally, on Wednesday, June 12, the final day of publication before the student editors moved to an abridged summer publishing schedule, the paper got around to acknowledging MSU's latest historical artifact.

Barely, though. The big stories that day were emblematic of the era: "Algerian Streets Scene of More French Riots," "Ike Returns to Office" after a short illness, and, in sports, "Stan the Man (Musial) Ties Mark for Consecutive Games." Andy Griffith was starring in *A Face in the Crowd* at the Gladmer Theater, and Audrey Hepburn was in *Funny Face* at the Lucon.

Finally, buried on page 8, the last page, was a small notice squeezed up against a mug shot of the new grim-looking head of Soviet economic planning. The small headline announced: "Locomotive Received as Museum Exhibit." And the story, in its entirety, read: "The gift of a steam locomotive to MSU was formally received from the Chesapeake & Ohio Railway Company Monday afternoon."

There was no mention of Monday's dignified ceremony, no mention of Cyrus Eaton's inspiration or Forest Akers's largesse, and certainly no mention of the place in mechanical history

◀ Michigan State University vice president Thomas Hamilton (*right*) and Chesapeake & Ohio general manager C. J. Milliken pose as the university takes the deed to its new display locomotive. Courtesy of Michigan State University Archives and Historical Collections.

held by that "steam locomotive," PM 1225. With a location on the fringe of campus, and news coverage on the fringe of the student newspaper, the new exhibit was just where Hannah wanted it.

❖   ❖   ❖

Despite its size, 1225 attracted little attention in its new role as a public monument. Enclosed by a chain-link fence topped by three strands of barbed wire, the locomotive was relatively safe from vandalism and became a hands-on exhibit on occasions when groups of twenty or more expressed interest in a tour. The university installed a formidable steel staircase leading up to both sides of the cab, and once inside visitors could gawk at all the gauges, the red valve handles, the moveable firedoors, and other marvels.

Although the modest enclosure provided only minimal security, the locked gates and automobile and student/pedestrian traffic on Stadium Road may have discouraged the sorts of thieves who descended on park engines across the country in the years immediately following dieselization. Unlike hundreds of other display locomotives, 1225 managed to retain all its key collectible accessories, such as the whistle and bell, the main steam gauge, the brass Lima builder's plates, and, most coveted of all, the number plate on the front of the smokebox.

There was one unfortunate incident, however: at some point pranksters started a fire on the grates of 1225's firebox. Figuring they were of no value, the university had the grates removed and discarded. Crews also permanently opened the firedoors with a welded steel spacer.

The Stadium Drive enclosure was inadequate for preservation of an outdoor park engine. Big and indestructible as they seem, steam locomotives quickly fall prey to the elements. The worst, of course, are rain and snow and the accumulated effects of rust. An aluminum cover was installed over the coal bunker of the tender, but other than that 1225 was at the mercy of the weather. Moreover, the asbestos lagging under the engine's boiler jacket had never been removed, and over the years this insulating material "held rainwater like a sponge, accelerating rust in all it touched," as 1225 historian David Jones has described.[3]

The engine also attracted its share of birds, insects, and even some vines. In the years to come, museum director Baker would attempt from time to time to get approval for a shelter, but it never happened. Estimates from MSU's Physical Plant division yielded three separate estimates ranging from $30,000 to $50,000, all of which the administration rejected. For the most part, the 1225's caretakers fulfilled Hannah's instruction to give it "minimum maintenance." The caretaking appeared to decline even more precipitously after Forest Akers's death in 1966 at age seventy-seven. Slowly, the locomotive acquired the patina common to virtually all park engines: dirt, rust, and guano.

But 1225 didn't remain completely out of the public eye. After 1960, its isolated corner of the MSU campus became a livelier place, thanks to the continued expansion of the university's residence-hall system, the largest in the nation. One by one, four huge dorms went up along Chestnut Road, just west of Stadium Road across from the football practice field. The first was Case Hall, opened in 1961, followed by Wilson Hall in 1962, Wonders Hall in 1963, and, finally, Holden Hall in 1967, the last major dorm built at MSU. Another development of apartments for married students had gone up west of Harrison Road in the late 1950s, including University Village and the huge Spartan Village.

In just a few years, a population of thousands of students had sprung up on the southwest side of the campus, many of them crossing Stadium Road and passing 1225 each day as they walked to class. Most probably ignored the huge black locomotive. But by 1969, 1225 had acquired a couple of especially ardent admirers. One was an Air Force Reserve Officers' Training Corps (ROTC) officer who loved railroads and had been volunteering to open up 1225's enclosure on weekends. The other was an electrical engineering major from Saginaw who lived over in married housing and had big ideas.

LEGACY OF THE CHESAPEAKE & OHIO KANAWHAS

When Chesapeake & Ohio (C&O) chairman Cyrus Eaton suggested to Forest Akers that Michigan State accept a decommissioned steam locomotive as a gift, he was making a familiar sales pitch. The C&O was bullish on preserving steam, even as it was sending hundreds of engines to the scrapper in the mid-to-late 1950s. In fact, the C&O can take credit for saving more examples of a single class of locomotive—the K-4 class 2-8-4—than any other major railroad.

Although perhaps not as famous as the Berkshires on the Nickel Plate (NKP) or Pere Marquette (PM), the Kanawhas (as the C&O dubbed its 2-8-4s) shared the same Advisory Mechanical Committee pedigree. From 1937 to 1947, the railroad ordered 129 of the engines, dividing the orders between Alco and Lima. More utilitarian in appearance than the PM and NKP engines, the C&O's 2-8-4s were heavier than their cousins and hauled larger tenders. They toiled in relative obscurity, mainly lugging coal out of the hollows of West Virginia and eastern Kentucky.

The legacy of the preserved Kanawhas is mixed. Many received cursory paint jobs and then were subjected to the elements. The "class engine" (so-called because it was the first to be built) was 2700, donated by the C&O to the city of Charleston, West Virginia, in 1955. Displayed for many years in the city's Coonskin Park, 2700 was gradually picked apart by vandals and became a symbol for how *not* to treat an artifact. Today the engine is at the Dennison Railroad Museum in Dennison, Ohio, where it faces a brighter future. Other lone K-4s include 2755 in West Virginia's Chief Logan State Park; 2756 in Huntington Park in Newport News, Virginia; 2760 in Riverside Park in Lynchburg, Virginia; and 2732 at the Science Museum of Virginia in Richmond.

Five of the Kanawhas ended up in the collections of major railroad museums, including 2727 at the National Museum of Transport in St. Louis; 2707 at the Illinois Railway Museum in Union, Illinois; 2705, which escaped the scrap line in 1975 to join the Baltimore & Ohio Railroad Museum in Baltimore; 2736 at the National Railroad Museum in Green Bay, Wisconsin; and 2716 at the Kentucky Railway Museum in New Haven, Kentucky.

The latter made a big splash in 1981–82 when Southern Railway leased and refurbished it for a few months of excursion service. Another K-4, 2789, for several years has been the subject of operating plans at the Hoosier Valley Railroad Museum in North Judson, Indiana.

That leaves 2776, which remains on display in Jesse Eyman Park in Washington Court House, Ohio. The locomotive is in relatively good condition, thanks to the ministrations of a dedicated caretaker who keeps the 2-8-4 cleaned and painted. It's a testimonial to the wisdom of the Advisory Mechanical Committee that 2776's grates still do the job they were designed for: supporting the fire inside PM 1225.

▶ Local boys clamber atop the smokebox of C&O 2700 during the 2-8-4's dedication in Coonskin Park in Charleston, West Virginia, in October 1955. Courtesy of *Trains* magazine collection.

CHAPTER 5

Students Take Up
a Cause

For much of the American college scene, 1969 was a season of discontent. Student protests had become routine, usually focused on the war in Vietnam but also on matters closer to home. In April, members of the Students for a Democratic Society (SDS) took over University Hall at Harvard, only to be forced out a few days later by police. In May, approximately 10,000 Indiana University students demonstrated and boycotted classes in a dispute over student fees. The worst episode came on May 15, "Bloody Thursday," at the University of California in Berkeley, where one student was killed and more than 125 hospitalized after police cleared the ad hoc "People's Park" area of the campus.

Michigan State University (MSU) had seen ferment as well, mostly in the form of a "Smash ROTC" movement on the campus. But little of that registered with Randy Paquette, a junior from Saginaw. Paquette was far too busy for politics, with his marriage that June to his high school sweetheart, Betty; his job working for the MSU Physical Plant as a student electrician; and his studies in electrical engineering. When he'd stay up late in apartment 1108-B at the University Village married-housing complex, it was only to plot his career.

But Paquette could be diverted. That September, he saw an article in the *State News*, MSU's daily newspaper, profiling another student named Steve Reeves, who was starting a railroad

◄ Running gear of the 1225, photographed at the Owosso Train Festival 2009. Private collection.

▶ In the first publicity photo taken for the Michigan State University Railroad Club, members take the first steps toward dismantling 1225 in 1970. From left are Steve Reeves, club president; Randy Paquette; and an unidentified member. Courtesy of Michigan State University Archives and Historical Collections.

▶ Project 1225 mechanical guru Randy Paquette uses a pneumatic chisel to remove staybolt caps from the outer firebox sheet on 1225's boiler. Photo by John B. Corns.

club on campus. Reeves worked for the MSU Museum, giving tours of the steam locomotive over on Stadium Road when weather permitted. Paquette knew the engine. While he wouldn't have described himself as a railroad fan, he loved machinery, and on his way to class he'd admired the giant example marked "Chesapeake & Ohio 1225."

"I'd grown up in Saginaw along a Grand Trunk Western branch, which had steam locomotives up until about 1960," Paquette later recalled. "My family told me that, as a kid, I'd wanted to be a locomotive engineer." In the *State News* story, Paquette noted that Reeves was starting up the MSU Railroad Club. He decided to go to a meeting.[1]

Reeves was the antithesis of the hirsute student protester. With his pressed slacks and his brush cut, he looked every bit the Reserve Officers' Training Corps (ROTC) officer he was.

Headed for graduation in 1972, he would move straight into an air force officer's commission. He was also an all-purpose railfan who liked model railroading and swore allegiance to the Santa Fe Railway. When he started the MSU Railroad Club, it was to share such interests with other railfans.

But Reeves's ideas for the club lasted only as long as it took Randy Paquette to show up. Paquette went to his first meeting at the MSU Union with one question in mind: why not restore 1225 and run the engine on football excursions?

Years later Reeves acknowledged that he was dismissive of the idea, for the obvious reason that it seemed impossible, even insane. A ragtag group of student railfans was hardly in a position to restore 220 tons of machinery. If cost and inexperience weren't good enough reasons, there were other contraindications. Everyone knew the locomotive had that bad pony-truck bearing, ruined when 1225 was delivered in 1957. Moreover, some had come to believe the locomotive's wheels must be flat after all those years of sitting under dead weight.

Paquette was undeterred, and gradually, as other students began joining the club, the crazy, romantic notion took hold. The mission was 1225. The goal was to put it back in service.

◆　　◆　　◆

The idea of running a large steam locomotive for fun wasn't insane. In 1970, there were scores of steam locomotives still operating across North America, mostly small engines at tourist railroads and museums. But steam fans also could ride behind large engines on main-line railroads. Most prominent was Union Pacific and its 4-8-4 No. 8444, a thoroughbred passenger engine built in 1944 by Alco and kept in service for trips out of Cheyenne, Wyoming. The Southern Railway had a stable of smaller engines it used across its system, most famous among them green-and-gold 2-8-2 No. 4501. A private locomotive owner, Dick Jensen of Chicago, had scattered success in Indiana and Michigan with trips behind his GTW 4-6-2 No. 5629.

If any locomotive directly inspired some members of the MSU Railroad Club, it was Nickel Plate (NKP) No. 759, one of those Van Sweringen/Advisory Mechanical Committee 2-8-4s so similar to 1225. After the NKP retired the engine in 1958, it wound up in the collection of

Steamtown, a museum in Bellows Falls, Vermont, launched by industrialist F. Nelson Blount. The 759 endured Vermont's weather for nearly a decade before being leased and rescued in 1968 by the High Iron Company, a New Jersey–based excursion promoter.

The 759 had the distinction of being the first large American steam locomotive brought back to service after static outdoor display. High Iron's owner, Ross Rowland, a successful Wall Street commodities broker, had excellent connections with a number of major railroads, and his exploits with 759 on high-profile trips across the Northeast and Midwest made a strong impression on some members of 1225's young crew.

However, any similarity between High Iron and the club was limited to the nearly identical profiles of their two machines. High Iron boasted a seasoned crew of locomotive mechanics and former railroaders, and they had restored 759 inside the old NKP roundhouse in Conneaut, with many of the necessary tools and equipment left over from the steam era. The effort was backed by Rowland's considerable fortune, his access to

▲ This UPI wire service telephoto dated August 13, 1970, was sent out to newspapers with the caption "Lansing: A young Michigan State Coed walks past the old 240-ton Pere Marquette steam locomotive [1225] which will undergo a complete rebuilding soon. With the blessings of MSU President Clifton R. Wharton Jr., the MSU Railroad Club will tackle the massive job to transport students as well as team members to selected football games and other MSU athletic events."

railroad managements, and his all-consuming ambition.

The 1225 club had none of that. No experience, no roundhouse, no roof, no tools, and, most of all, no money. The odds against the club getting anywhere were staggering. Steam locomotives were designed to be maintained in roundhouse stalls and huge erecting halls; attended to by armies of machinists, pipefitters, and boilermakers; and supported by lathes and jacks and wheelset drop pits every bit as ponderous as the locomotives themselves. Removing even the smallest accessory from an engine usually called for an overhead crane.

And then there was the cost. Rebuilding 1225 would require expensive and increasingly rare industrial skills: certified boilermakers for the boiler; running-gear experts to restore the bearings and rods; machinists to tear down and rebuild pumps, tanks, generators, and scores of other appurtenances large and small; and sheet-metal workers to manufacture a new boiler jacket and other parts. Someone would have to manage the entire affair.

In the March 1971 inaugural edition of its

▶ High Iron Company's Nickel Plate 759, a close cousin to 1225 and an early inspiration for the Michigan State University Railroad Club, thunders down the Norfolk & Western main line at Natural Bridge, Virginia, with a November 1968 excursion. Photo by Don Wood, courtesy of *Trains* magazine collection.

newsletter, *Project 1225*, the club members gamely predicted they would raise $30,000 to get 1225 running. They'd do it with membership dues, sale of chrome-plated railroad spikes, and random donations. The only problem was that, in 1971, the restoration of a locomotive the size of 1225 typically cost twenty or thirty times that goal, probably more. Running a big steam engine was a million-dollar proposition.

Undaunted, the students plowed ahead. "We were all young and impressionable," recalls Aarne Frobom, one of the earliest members of the club. "We didn't know enough to be aware of what we were getting into, so we just tore into it, and tried to make sense of it ever since." And if their faith wasn't enough, they could rely on three angels to help get them where they were going.

◆   ◆   ◆

The first angel was Rollin Baker, the director of the MSU Museum. Baker already had a cordial relationship with Reeves via the weekend tours of the engine. As a part of the museum's collection, 1225 was the largest artifact in Baker's charge, and Reeves and this new railroad club provided the museum some assurance the locomotive would be kept in reasonably good condition.

But restoring the big hulk on Stadium Road to operating condition was a different proposition, and Baker wouldn't seem predisposed to support such a project. A zoologist and mammalogist by profession, he grew up in Texas and became an internationally recognized expert on Mexican mammals. Most of all he was a scientist whose main job was to advance the MSU Museum's basic mission to interpret natural history. The science of Super Power steam wasn't part of the deal.

And yet, over the years, Baker watched out for the welfare of 1225. He regarded seriously the locomotive's place in mechanical history. He was also a charming, approachable man who loved students, even these misfits so dedicated to a steam locomotive. Baker met early on with Reeves and Paquette and gave the club's project his blessing.

In the years to come, he would be called on often to run interference for the project when it provoked the ire of the university's administration. In that role, he became an indispensable friend to 1225. In an interview with the *Lansing State Journal*, he seemed to have a soft spot for 1225. "The engine isn't of much value to anyone right now. It makes no academic contribution, and the engineering departments aren't interested in ancient, old-fashioned machinery." But he may have realized that the locomotive had a lot to teach.

Baker's influence was obvious when, on August 6, 1970, an MSU press release cheerfully reported that the club had the blessings of the university's new president, Clifton R. Wharton Jr. The press release said, "Randy Paquette, Saginaw senior majoring in electrical engineering, and a prime mover in the club, explains that once the locomotive is operative it is expected to be self-supporting and will be run on a nonprofit basis."

◆   ◆   ◆

In the spring of 1971, with Baker's blessing, the fledgling club turned to doing some actual work on Project 1225. But without tools or facilities, club members couldn't get very far. The intrepid Paquette, however, found another angel.

It's impossible to imagine 1225 running today without Don Childs, who had the title of supervisor in the Division of Engineering Research at MSU. What that really meant was that he ran MSU's expansive machine shop in the basement of the Engineering building, only a block or so away from the locomotive. An unassuming, upbeat man, Childs took kindly to the idea of restoring 1225 when Paquette first approached him in the fall of 1970. Childs made the key decision to allow club members, under his direct supervision, to begin working on locomotive parts in his shop.

Childs wasn't a member of the MSU faculty, but he should have been. He had an all-encompassing knowledge of things mechanical, everything from welding to machining to electrical repair. He also knew instinctively how to teach, and he did it with encouragement and patience. Club members came to see him as a mentor, and Childs treated his apprentices like star students. He also liked the idea that working on a locomotive was a positive alternative to protesting.

Don Childs, one of Project 1225's earliest champions, ran the machine shop for Michigan State University's Engineering Department. Courtesy of Steam Railroading Institute collection.

▲ With the help of Michigan State University's power-plant crane, crews remove the sandbox from atop 1225's boiler, already shorn of much of its jacket. Photo by John B. Corns.

One of Childs's most important interns was Chuck Julian, a geology major from Pontiac whose family owned a foundry. Julian had an aptitude for all things mechanical, especially when it came to welding, and he would go on to make a number of unique technical and financial contributions to Project 1225. He is unabashed in his admiration for his tutor. "Don Childs made the restoration possible," says Julian.[2]

By the spring of 1971, a series of important parts off 1225 began rotating in and out of Childs's shop. First was the dynamo, a steam-powered generator that provides electricity for all the locomotive's running lights. Soon came the stoker control assembly, which ran the auger that loaded coal into the firebox, then the low-water alarm, a key safety device.

Most of those smaller parts could be taken off the engine with winches and chains and hauled over to the shop in the back of a truck. But more elaborate measures were required for 1225's two massive 1,200-pound Westinghouse air compressors, 8½-by-12-inch pumps that drove all the air systems, including the engine and train brakes. The ponderous pumps, as well as the huge sandbox atop the boiler, were removed from 1225 in the summer of 1972 using the university's 25-ton crane from the Shaw Lane power plant.

Paquette later secured a tow truck to carry the pumps over to the machine shop and lower them into an access bay. One of the pumps dropped, breaking off one of its mounts, which went shooting across the shop floor like an artillery shell. In a teaching moment later, Childs helped Julian learn how to weld the part back on, with some help from a welding-rod salesman. Julian would go on to make rebuilding both pumps a personal project.

The club got some good news in April 1972 when it inspected the damaged bearing on 1225's pony truck. Using three 100-ton jacks borrowed from the university, the crew lifted the front of the engine 2 inches and removed the burned-out bearing. With the help of Gordon Luscher, a retired Pere Marquette (PM) engine inspector from Wyoming, the team determined the wheelset itself hadn't been damaged. All that was needed was a replacement 6½-by-12-inch bearing.

With most of the external parts removed, the crew began the dirty job of removing the old boiler jacket and disposing of the asbestos insulation, called "lagging." It was a tricky operation. Because of uncertainty as to when and how the jacket might be replaced, each large section of sheet steel had to marked and stored. In an operation that today would be patently illegal, members tore off the loose chunks of lagging and threw them into a dumpster behind the engine. Restrictions on the industrial use of asbestos were nearly a decade away; fortunately, 1225's lagging was damp and unlikely to become airborne.

Drivers and pedestrians surely noticed that the locomotive was creating an entirely new visual impression: rust. The removal of the shiny black jacket and lagging exposed a boiler covered in a coat of light orange, most of it innocuous but none of it appealing. For the sake of the boiler and the image of the project, club members spent several weeks scraping rust before painting the entire surface with black DeRustO.

▲ Retired Pere Marquette roundhouse foreman Herschel Christensen checks 1225's water glass, which monitors the water level in the boiler. Club member Roger Scovill looks on. Photo by John B. Corns.

▲ Sam Chidester, retired Pere Marquette locomotive engineer, sits in a familiar seat. The veteran recalled 1225 as an "average" member of the N-1 class of 2-8-4s. Photo by John B. Corns.

On a splendid September day in 2009, 1225 and 765 perform together on a freight train at Bannister, Michigan.
PHOTO BY MITCH GOLDMAN.

◄ The 765 leads 1225 over the New River at the remote Chesapeake and Ohio junction point of Sewell, West Virginia, August 10, 1991.
PHOTO BY KEVIN P. KEEFE.

Its power reduced because of a siphon leak, 1225 follows 765 as the engines perform at Thurmond, West Virginia, on August 10, 1991. ►
PHOTO BY H. E. BROUSE.

◄ Sunlight bathes the Michigan Bean elevator at Henderson during a September 2009 photo freight charter.
PHOTO BY MITCH GOLDMAN.

The old New Buffalo turntable goes to work at its new location at the Steam Railroading Institute, turning the 2-8-4 for another run. ►
PHOTO BY JEFF MAST.

It's dusk as the two Van Sweringen Berkshires perform on a photo freight at Smith's Crossing near Owosso in September 2009.
PHOTO BY MITCH GOLDMAN.

◄ A column of coal smoke looms over the grain elevator at Carland during a North Pole Express trip in December 2013.
PHOTO BY JEFF MAST.

The dusk of late winter casts a cold light on 1225 during a photo freight charter in March 2008. ►
PHOTO BY M. ROSS VALENTINE.

PERE MARQUETTE 1225

▲ A panned photo of 1225 taken near Owosso in February 2008 shows the classic profile of the AMC-designed Berkshire.
PHOTO BY MITCH GOLDMAN.

◄ Snow explodes as 1225's pilot hits a snowbank at a grade crossing near Henderson on December 20, 2008.
PHOTO BY M. ROSS VALENTINE.

◄ Crew members in classic trainmen's garb help create a timeless scene as 1225 rides the Owosso turntable at night.
PHOTO BY JEFF MAST.

Temporarily lettered "Polar Express," 1225 whistles past a grade crossing near Owosso in December 2004. ►
PHOTO BY M. ROSS VALENTINE.

◄ Vintage vehicles join 1225 to create an early 1950s scene at Owosso's former Grand Trunk Western depot in February 2008.

PHOTO BY MITCH GOLDMAN.

Nickel Plate and Pere Marquette 2-8-4s meet at the Owosso turntable during Train Festival 2014. ►

PHOTO BY JEFF MAST.

◄ Ignoring the laws of physics, the movie 1225 heaves to its side during a wild ride across an ice floe on its way to the North Pole.

His left hand on the throttle, engineer Greg Udolf maneuvers 1225 through the yard switches at Owosso. ▼

PHOTO BY JEFF MAST.

An iconic view of the animated 1225 shows how *The Polar Express* movie was faithful to the original book by including a recessed headlight and pronounced "cowcatcher." ▶

Trademark of Lima Locomotive Works: the distinctive diamond builder's plate at the front of 1225's smokebox. ▼

PHOTO BY JEFF MAST.

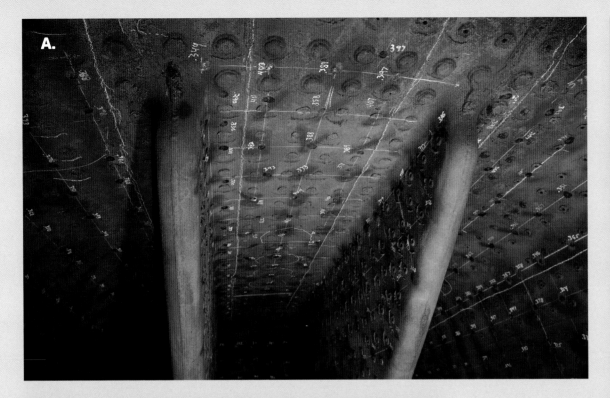

A. This interior view of the firebox shows thermic syphons descending from the crownsheet; chalk marks indicate upcoming firebox work.

B. A photo taken from inside the boiler looking forward shows 1225's large "dry pipe" (*top*), which collects steam at the top of the boiler.

C. Inside the smokebox, steam collects in the superheater manifold (*center*) and is delivered to the cylinders via two huge steam delivery pipes.

PHOTOS BY JEFF MAST.

Around this time, some retired PM veterans began showing up at the site with some regularity. They included Luscher, the engine inspector; Sam Chidester, a locomotive engineer with plenty of experience on the PM 2-8-4s and who claimed to have broken in 1225 in 1941; and Herschel Christensen, retired roundhouse foreman and engine inspector from Grand Rapids. Chidester mostly shared colorful anecdotes—he recalled 1225 as a "rough ride"—but Christensen had more practical advice. "He assured us the wheels would not go flat sitting there on display," Paquette recalls.[3]

Life on weekends at the enclosure began to take on a routine. Usually at least a handful of club members would show up, some to pursue a loosely organized list of mechanical projects, some to take turns showing visitors around. The crew was fueled by doughnuts in the morning from a convenience store on Trowbridge Road, and at lunch by a run to McDonald's. Attentive visitors might have heard members exhort each other with the unofficial slogan of Project 1225: "It'll never run."

◆   ◆   ◆

As the commotion grew around the display site, the club began to attract new members, and weekend work sessions became crowded inside the enclosure. A problem quickly arose: there was nowhere to store the organization's growing collection of tools and equipment, most of which were stuffed into the locomotive cab and the coal bunker and locked on Sunday night. The situation was aggravated by the theft of $420 worth of tools from the cab, later recovered along a street at the south edge of campus.

The club managed to raise enough money to keep the low-budget operation going. Initially the fund-raising consisted of club dues, first from students and later from nonstudent "associate" members around the country who supported the effort. Club members tried to attract interest by cheekily writing the number "1225" in chalk on sidewalks and classroom chalkboards and putting up "Free 1225" signs. One weekend they tried to raise funds by showing the old movie *Captain Marvel* in an Engineering lecture hall. On fall weekends, the

WATCH YOUR MONEY GO UP IN SMOKE!

Just five bucks. You can call it an investment....in Superpower. The Superpower of ex-Pere Marquette Berkshire No.1225, now being re—stored for mainline service at Michigan State University. Five dollars buys you a membership in Project 1225, gets you the newsletter, and gives you discounts on sales items and eventual trip tickets. Best of all, it puts you on the ground floor of big steam. But hurry! Reflueing has begun, and we need your help now!

Send your dues and contributions to:
The MSU Railroad Club, Project 1225
MSU Museum, E. Lansing, MI 48823

group brought out borrowed red Salvation Army buckets to solicit donations from fans streaming toward Spartan Stadium.[4]

One of the first important revenue streams took hold in April 1972 when the club ran its first advertisements in *Trains* magazine, the nation's leading rail enthusiast magazine. The ad came about after members met one night in Alison Potter's McDonel Hall dorm room to discuss marketing strategy. Potter was an advertising major. The team conceived a slogan that was as clever as it was straightforward: "Watch Your Money Go Up in Smoke."

The ads in *Trains* were only a third of a page (at about $250, all the club could afford) and were a frank appeal for help, but they worked, helping the club attract another sixty associate members and boosting the total membership roster to 275, many of whom

◄ The Michigan State University Railroad Club raised money with this ad in the April 1973 issue of *Trains.* Courtesy of *Trains* magazine collection.

In a 1973 photo used by the Michigan State University Railroad Club for national publicity, the Project 1225 crew poses amid the overall commotion of the display site. Photo by John B. Corns.

would stick with Project 1225 for decades to come. That March, the club was encouraged to hear that the Michigan House had endorsed the restoration in the form of a resolution of commendation.

◆　◆　◆

The modest flow of money helped, but the project couldn't get much further without an improved workspace. The necessary collection of tools and equipment had outgrown 1225's enclosure. The only power available was via a 400-foot extension cord plugged surreptitiously into the nearest campus building. Installing a temporary building at the site was out of the question, though; MSU's buildings and grounds department would never allow it. The answer, the club decided, was to find a suitable railroad car and park it next to the locomotive. A baggage car would certainly do. So could a Railway Post Office, commonly called an RPO.

Fortunately, there were plenty of both kinds of cars available in the summer of 1971. Amtrak had taken over a third of the national passenger-train service and canceled most of

◄ The Michigan State University Railroad Club's Railway Post Office car, so galling to MSU's administration, is parked adjacent to the locomotive in view of the work site. Photo by John B. Corns.

the rest on May 1. It launched its fleet by choosing 1,200 of the best cars among the thousands more offered by railroads shedding passenger service. Suddenly there was a huge supply of surplus coaches, sleepers, dining cars, and other rolling stock.

Members of the club figured a good source might be the Grand Trunk Western (GTW), whose tracks passed only a few hundred yards south of 1225. The GTW, or the Trunk, as it was known, had operated a schedule of good passenger trains right up until Amtrak Day and stored most of its leftover cars at its sprawling yard in Battle Creek. Paquette made an inquiry, and the GTW said "come on down."

On a sunny day in July, Paquette and two other members headed to Battle Creek to go shopping. After looking over several cars, they settled on RPO 9683, a handsome riveted-side heavyweight car built in 1914 by American Car & Foundry as GTW 36. It was painted in the black-and-white livery of the GTW's parent company, Canadian National. The club liked the fact that 9683 had roller bearings on all the axles of its six-wheel trucks. Moreover, its scores of cubbyholes and built-in workspaces for RPO clerks seemed perfect for storing tools and working on small projects. Best of all was the price: $500, F.O.B. East Lansing.

Michigan State University vice president Jack Breslin was devoted to maintaining the beauty of the campus, and an old Railway Post Office car wasn't part of the plan. Courtesy of Michigan State University Archives and Historical Collections.

Although the club had limited standing as a student organization, its check was good enough for the GTW, and the railroad dutifully complied with the instruction to "send it to MSU." The Railroad Club was the customer, not MSU, so a few months later, on the club's authority, the GTW dropped off the RPO at the Trowbridge interchange track, after which a Chesapeake & Ohio (C&O) switcher moved the car onto the spur next to 1225, just short of an old coal-hopper car stored near the locomotive. Suddenly, cars passing on Shaw Lane had a good view of an antique mail car.

It didn't take long for the university to react. No matter how historic the car was, the administration was not amused to have another piece of railroad equipment join the general mess over on Stadium Road. In this case, the only administrator who really mattered was Jack Breslin.

Breslin wasn't someone the club wanted to cross. As vice president of administration and public affairs, he was one of the most powerful people on campus, more of a hands-on force than the scholarly President Wharton. It was no exaggeration to call Breslin an MSU legend. He'd been associated with the university for thirty years, going back to his days as captain of the Spartans football team in 1945, when he was named most valuable player. He earned letters in both baseball and basketball. In 1989, MSU would ratify Breslin's legacy by putting his name on its new $45 million athletic arena; Breslin died in 1988 at age sixty-eight.

Not long after the RPO's arrival, Randy Paquette got called into the administration building to confront an irritated Breslin. "I got yelled at, no question about it," recalls Paquette. "I had to promise him we'd keep the car in good condition, and pledge that the arrangement wouldn't be permanent." In reality, Paquette had no idea how long the "arrangement" would last. A subsequent communication from Breslin indicated that if the project ground to a halt, 1225 would be cut up immediately. As if to make his point, the old coal-hopper car at the end of the spur soon was scrapped, unannounced. The club got the message.

◆　　◆　　◆

With the arrival of the RPO, installation of a generator, and continued restoration of smaller parts and systems in the MSU machine shop, attention inevitably turned to the most critical part of the locomotive, the boiler. Club members knew that eventually it would require major work and that finding the right person to repair it—and the money to pay for his services—wouldn't be easy. The project needed a certified boilermaker, preferably one familiar with steam locomotives. Several were known to the club, all associated either with other locomotives or generally available for hire at onerous market rates.

Then, one day in 1972, one of the retired PM railroaders who regularly visited mentioned the name of Ken Pelton, a certified boilermaker reportedly still on the C&O's payroll in Wyoming and presumably old enough to have worked on the 1200s. Little else was known about him.

A group of members decided to learn more about this mysterious boilermaker, and, with

Paquette in charge, a small delegation drove to the Wyoming shops one night to see if they could find him. The trip was memorable. Proceeding only on rumor and without any advance arrangements, the group simply drove onto C&O railroad property, ignored the "No Trespassing" signs, parked near the old main shop, and walked in the first door they could find.

Those who were there recall a haunting scene. Only a portion of the cavernous erecting hall was in use, and there was no second shift, so the place was mostly quiet. The lights inside threw a soft glow over a vast floor populated by machinery and a couple of diesel locomotives. The place smelled like oil and welding, much as it did when steam engines populated the building a quarter-century before. Every few moments the silence was interrupted by the low-frequency groan of huge air compressors off in some distant corner of the complex.

The students found the door to a locker room and, inside, met up with a few railroaders taking a coffee break. Other than being surprised at confronting a handful of callow intruders at ten o'clock at night, the men were friendly. Most important, they confirmed that, yes, Ken Pelton still worked for the railroad, and he was still a boilermaker, charged with taking care of all the pressure vessels in C&O's Northern Region, including the huge power plant boilers that gave Wyoming life. They also indicated how the group could get in touch with him.

Speeding back to the MSU campus that night along I-96, the delegation agreed: Ken Pelton sounded like the man they needed. He just might be another angel.

◄ With its boiler jacket removed, 1225 wears a plastic shroud to protect it from the elements in this January 1972 scene. Photo by John B. Corns.

THE UNLIKELY ALLY

Of all the people who were critical to saving the 1225, none was more important than Rollin H. Baker, the endlessly patient Michigan State University (MSU) Museum director who not only fought to take care of the university's rusting display locomotive but also later ran interference for the headstrong student club that dismantled it. "Dr. Baker was our most important benefactor and protector," says Chuck Julian, a key figure in the MSU Railroad Club's Project 1225. "Without his approval, the project would never have gotten off the ground."[5]

In fact, Julian, who was president of the club when the project nearly came to a halt in 1975, says Baker defended the club at considerable personal risk. "Vice President Jack Breslin was not a fan of the 1225 and had let it be known that any university employee who allowed a bunch of students to embarrass him with a highly visible project might be fired," Julian recalls. "Dr. Baker said that he fully understood what we wanted to do but, in his opinion, he would rather MSU be known for something other than campus anti-war protests."

There was nothing in Rollin Baker's background to suggest he'd someday risk his career for a steam locomotive. A renowned scientist and beloved professor, he had an international reputation as a mammalogist.

When he came to MSU in 1955 to run the museum, he also assumed professorships in two academic departments, zoology and fisheries and wildlife. He wrote scores of articles and books on a wide range of biogeographical and natural history subjects.

Baker was born in Illinois in 1916 but grew up in Texas, and his home state informed every aspect of his career. In 1937, he earned a B.A. in zoology from the University of Texas, where he was a member of the championship swim team. He received his M.S. in entomology from Texas A&M in 1938, followed by a Ph.D. in zoology from the University of Kansas in 1948. An early stint as a game biologist with the Texas Game, Fish, and Oyster Commission confirmed Baker's love of fieldwork, according to an encomium to Baker, published in 2009 at the University of Nebraska–Lincoln: "It was probably in rural Texas that Rollin developed his immense people skills—a feature of his personality that endeared him to strangers, friends, students, and colleagues."

Baker's fieldwork took a personal turn when, in 1939, he married Mary Waddell, the daughter of a game warden from Eagle Lake, Texas. Together the Bakers had a daughter, Elizabeth Alice, and two sons, Bruce Rollin and Byron Laurence.

Baker enlisted in the navy in 1943 and served on a submarine-chasing destroyer in the North Atlantic. Later in the war he was transferred to the South Pacific, where he was part of a navy medical research unit that conducted research on zoonotic diseases threatening island-hopping ground forces.

After the war, Baker won his first academic position at the University of Kansas, where he became the curator of mammals at the Museum of Natural History. It was at Kansas where he earned the nickname "Hoot" Baker after a field trip in which he misidentified an owl's carcass as a pheasant and suggested his team fry up the bird for breakfast. The University of Kansas student newspaper ran a story with the headline "Professor Eats Owl," and the nickname stuck.

Baker moved to MSU in 1955, not only to run the museum but also to launch nearly twenty years of important research on small mammals, often involving research trips to Mexico. He also wrote an important book on Michigan mammals. His tenure at the museum was remembered fondly by his successor, Kurt Dewhurst. "He touched many students' lives in lasting ways as they found academic and curatorial positions and often work in state DNR departments," wrote Dewhurst. "We always appreciated his remarkable broad range of interests including literature, politics, sports, and his lively sense of humor."[6]

Although the MSU Museum had very little stake in America's mechanical history, Rollin Baker saw something valuable in having 1225 in the museum's collection, and he worked hard to care for the engine in the years leading up to Project 1225. In the end, club members came to admire him as much as his graduate students did. "Once the project got going, we owed it to Dr. Baker to make sure the project kept going to completion, even though early on we didn't know the peril that he put himself in by allowing us to attempt a restoration," says Julian. "I have great respect and admiration for him."[7]

After retiring from MSU in 1982, Baker moved back to Eagle Lake, Texas. He was still working on journal articles when he died on November 12, 2007, one day after his ninety-first birthday.

▶ Michigan State University Museum director Rollin H. Baker, a friend of 1225 and renowned among mammal researchers, poses with a friend. Courtesy of Michigan State University Archives and Historical Collections.

CHAPTER 6

Firing It Up

From the moment the Michigan State University (MSU) Railroad Club began taking parts off 1225, members knew that earnestness could only take them so far. No matter how many old railroaders they talked to, or old steam manuals they read, or hunks of metal they sandblasted, eventually they would need a professional. Everything they'd done so far was nibbling around the edges of the central challenge looming over them behind that chain-link fence: 1225's massive boiler.

The 1225's boiler carried the pedigree of the Lima-built, Advisory Mechanical Committee–designed Berkshire. But even the best boilers are, in the end, cantankerous and potentially dangerous pressure vessels, subject to withering stresses on the road. The 1225's boiler carried 7,000 gallons of water. In full operating mode, it converted water to steam at the rate of 66,584 pounds per hour, developing a boiler horsepower of 3,201. On the road, the boiler required the constant vigilance of engineer and fireman. In the shop, it required the expert ministrations of the boilermaker.

The best boilermakers were cool cats, mindful of the high stakes of their work even as they applied their skills at welding and metallurgy. The International Brotherhood of Boilermakers puts it this way: "Boilermakers have always worked under, in, and around high pressure. That

◄ Preparing for an eventual fireup, the MSU crew works inside 1225's boiler on May 11, 1974. Visible behind the firebox flue sheet are Pete Camps (*left*) and boilermaker Ken Pelton. The first five rebuilt flues are visible in the right foreground. Photo by John B. Corns.

is the nature of making boilers."[1] In the boiler profession, pressure is as much figurative as it is literal.

For Project 1225 to be successful, the club required a practiced, steady hand. By all indications, Ken Pelton could be that man. But how to recruit him? What were the chances he'd be willing to crawl around another cramped, dank boiler after doing the same thing all week for the railroad? How could the club possibly afford him? The crew wasn't even entirely certain he'd worked on Pere Marquette's Berkshires. And if so, after twenty-two years, would he remember enough about them to do the job effectively?

The job of contacting Pelton fell to the reliable Randy Paquette. Not long after the visit to Wyoming, Paquette tracked down the boilermaker's home phone number and called him, cold turkey. Would Pelton possibly be willing to work on 1225? He said he'd be willing to listen, so Paquette planned a quick trip to Pelton's home in Allegan.

◆　◆　◆

The success of an unlikely endeavor often turns on the intersection of special people and serendipitous moments. Maybe it was the audacity of the club's request, or maybe it was Randy Paquette's personable manner, or maybe the man was just having a good day, but Pelton took Paquette's request under consideration, thought about it for a few days, and agreed to give Project 1225 a try.

You could look high and low across the landscape of the American railroad and never find someone as perfect for the 1225 job as Pelton. Preternaturally cheerful, he'd started out with the Pere Marquette at Wyoming in 1941, giving him a solid ten years on the Berkshires. He had since perfected his craft on all manner of stationary boilers, large and small, as well as on the Chesapeake & Ohio's fleet of steam ferries. Now, nearing retirement, he was something of a legend around the Wyoming shops. He also loved young people: Pelton was active in the Boy Scouts. It's not hard to imagine he saw the 1225 crew as another Scout troop.

Pelton's arrangement with the club was ideal. He agreed to do whatever boiler work was

necessary for free, providing the club would
cover all his travel costs from his home
115 miles to the west. But even that was a
gift—Ken Pelton and his wife, Wauneta, loved
to travel in their truck camper. If visits to
work on the engine in East Lansing required
an overnight stay, they'd simply stay in their
truck.

Before Pelton could tackle the major
issue facing the boiler—the tubes and
flues—the club put him to work replacing
hundreds of staybolt caps. The locomotive
has 3,174 rigid and flexible staybolts that hold
together the internal and external sheets
of the firebox. A flexible staybolt has a ball
seat on the outer sheet, allowing for slight
movement of the firebox, and each ball end
is sealed by a hemispherical cap. Most of
1225's caps were badly pitted and in need of
replacement.

As Pelton went to work in the fall of
1972, club members were in awe, as Aarne
Frobom noted in the October–November
issue of *Project 1225*: "Ken has spent much of
his time already teaching and advising our
younger mechanics in the ways of steam and

▲ Boilermaker Ken Pelton, who worked on Pere
Marquette 2-8-4s, rolls flues in 1225's firebox,
accompanied by member Pete Camps, in a May 1974
photo. Photo by John B. Corns.

steel, much as the ancient master sculptors passed on their knowledge of stone and clay to eager apprentices."

All along, the club suspected that 1225's boiler would need substantial repairs. How much was unclear without conducting an inspection and hydrostatic test, which involves filling the entire boiler with water pushed to 15 percent beyond normal operating pressure. The pressurized water exposes leaks in the flues, tubes, and boiler but is entirely safe: since water is nearly incompressible, it releases only a negligible amount of energy if it forces a leak, unlike the explosive power of a boiler under steam. Since 1225's front and rear flue sheets looked clean, there was some hope the hydro test would show they would not require a lot of work.

The club scheduled the test for November 4, 1972. Using only the garden hose from the Landscape Architecture building, filling the boiler with 5,000 gallons of water would be an ordeal. Once again, improvisation was the order of the day. Paquette made an appeal to the East Lansing Fire Department, which dispatched a classic Mack pumper to help fill the engine.

Alas, as the test got under way, the water pressure climbed to only 100 pounds before Pelton discovered serious leaks coming from two of the flues at the front sheet. Further analysis indicated all the flues would have to be removed. A disappointed Paquette was philosophical. "We knew there would have to be surgery," he said. "We didn't know it would have to be major."

Major surgery wasn't all bad news. Removal of the flues would allow for inspection of the interior of the boiler as required by Federal Railroad Administration (FRA) rules. Early in 1973 the club plunged ahead. First to come out of the boiler were 1225's fifty-two Type E superheater units, which are bundles of $1\frac{3}{16}$–inch, return-bend steel tubing placed inside the flues to dry the steam before it goes to the throttle and cylinders, absorbing another 400 degrees in temperature. Stretched end to end the tubes would be 8,129 feet long. The superheaters would require repairs of their own, but for the time being they were stored in rented space at an industrial center in Lansing.

▶ During the November 1972 hydrostatic test of 1225's boiler, Ken Pelton welds leaky staybolts. Assisting Pelton is member Jerry Willson. Photo by John B. Corns.

Next up were the flues. Removing them was something members could do themselves, without Pelton, so Paquette bought a pair of 3 and 3½–inch Weideke flue cutters at $1,100 apiece. The tools worked on the rear flue sheet, but not in front in the smokebox, so Chuck Julian cut the flues out with a torch. The crew removed the first flue on February 10 and by April had removed all 275. It was an arduous task. Each flue was 19 feet long and heavy, requiring two people to pull it out from the smokebox and carry it to a storage rack, where each tube was individually hydro tested.

For the 1225 crew, the repetitive manual labor was its own history lesson. "It has become painfully obvious why the railroads deserted the steam locomotive," observed Frobom. "The labor and maintenance involved is amazing."[2]

The club decided to salvage as much of each flue as possible by using a procedure from steam days called safe-ending. Flue defects were most common at each end where the tube was welded into the flue sheet. To preserve most of each flue, Pelton could weld a short extension at each end, permissible under FRA boiler regulations.

While the flue project continued, the crew also cleaned up 1225's American Multiple Valve Throttle, a huge assembly at the front of the boiler that gathered steam from the superheaters in a large manifold and delivered it to the power cylinders. Members also disassembled and cleaned the injector and feedwater heater, which deliver water from the tender to 1225's boiler.

The hard work on the engine was suspended briefly for social reasons on the weekend of May 12, 1973. The year before, the club had begun the tradition of an annual spring banquet and had as its speaker Donald D. Smith, an official of the High Iron Company. For 1973, the club swung for the fences, inviting the biggest media star in railroading, David P. Morgan, the veteran editor of *Trains* magazine. Morgan surprised the club by saying "yes" and came to East Lansing to deliver a rousing speech.

◆   ◆   ◆

Work on the engine slowed down over the summer. First, MSU union employees went on strike for three weeks, slowing deliveries and halting work at the MSU Machine Shop. Also, a strike at

◄ Chuck Julian (*left*) and an unidentified club member work on the front flue sheet inside 1225's firebox. Courtesy of Steam Railroading Institute collection.

American Boiler Tube Company in McKees Rocks, Pennsylvania, delayed the delivery of the safe-ends for the flues. The club did manage to order arch brick from a company in Missouri, using the same molds used to supply Nickel Plate 759 back in 1968. Arch bricks are made of a refractory material and are suspended between arch tubes above the fire, improving combustion by forcing the hot gases to circulate to the back of the firebox before charging forward through the flues.

The summer slowdown brought news of another Van Sweringen 2-8-4. Down in Fort Wayne, Indiana, 128 miles south of East Lansing, a new group was making arrangements to cosmetically restore Nickel Plate No. 765, which had been on display outdoors in Fort Wayne since 1963. The Fort Wayne Railroad Historical Society (FWRHS) was formed by Nickel Plate fans in 1972.

▶ The work zone around 1225 is strewn with equipment during the May 17, 1975, hydrostatic test of the locomotive's boiler. Photo by John B. Corns.

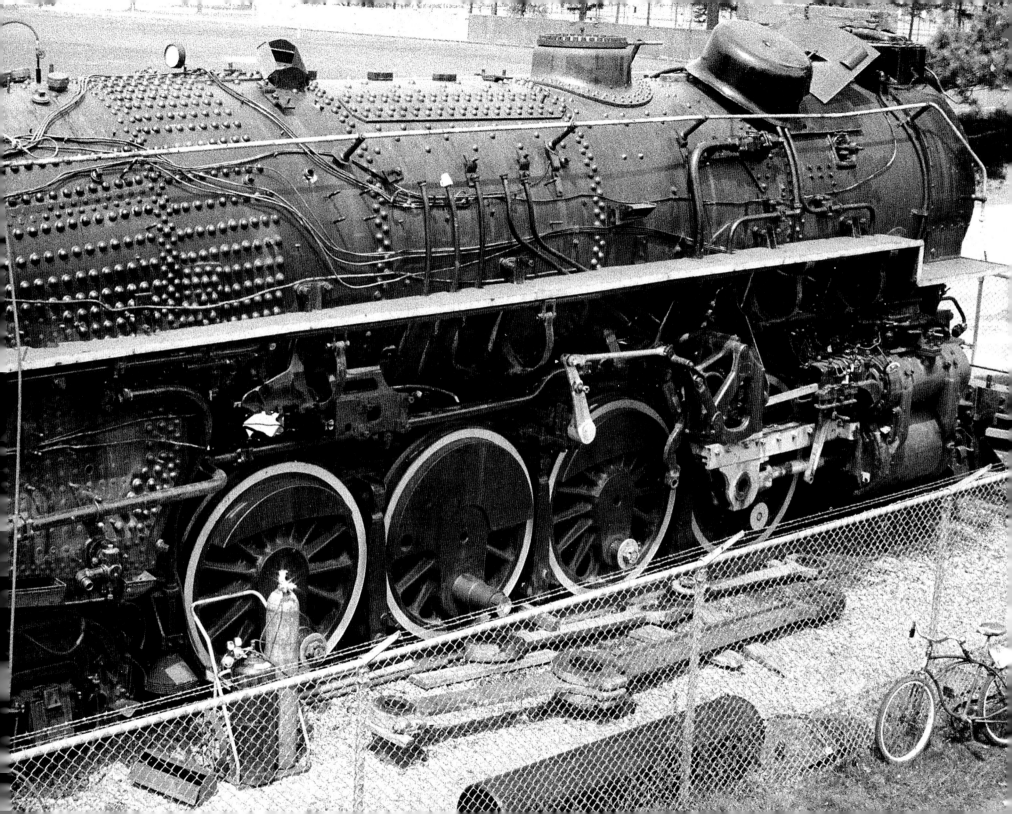

For most who get involved with steam, cosmetic makeovers are never enough, and the 765 project quickly morphed into a full-scale restoration. The FWRHS secured a long-term lease of the engine from the city and made arrangements to move to a new building in New Haven, on Fort Wayne's east side. The society recruited a group of supporters and volunteers from across Indiana and Ohio, some of them with experience in the main-line steam excursion business. By 1974, the rebuilding of 765 was well under way.

Given the similarities of 1225 and 765, it was only natural that the East Lansing and Fort Wayne organizations struck up a fruitful relationship, sharing information and expertise and occasionally making visits to each other's restoration site. If there was any sense of competition, it wasn't obvious. The two locomotives' paths would cross a number of times in the years to come, with spectacular results.

◆　　◆　　◆

Ken Pelton got going on the boiler in earnest over the rest of 1973 and into 1974, and his work was an inspiration to his apprentices. Whenever his weekends allowed, he'd make the trek to East Lansing and park overnight near the locomotive. One by one, with his team of helpers, he safe-ended and reinstalled each of the 275 flues and tubes. By October 1974, the job was completed. The club calculated the team had performed 6,000 separate operations involving cutting, testing, rolling, beading, welding, and other tasks.

Next it was time to test Pelton's work. Unusually warm weather on January 25, 1975, allowed the club to finally stage a successful hydro. Workers began filling the boiler on Friday, and member David Jones stayed up with the engine all night, ready to drain the boiler if it appeared the temperature would dip below freezing. The weather held, and on Saturday the crew cranked up the pressure to 315 psi. The boiler passed, exhibiting only a few easily repairable leaks. It appeared there was clear sailing to a fireup.

Meanwhile, 1225 needed a set of grates. You can't put a fire in a firebox without them. The university's decision to remove them back in the 1960s now seemed particularly rash. One option was to use the grates in Pere Marquette 1223, on display at the State Fair in Detroit. Given the limited prospects for 1223, the club was shocked when fair officials said "no." So they sought alternative sources.

The club's new friends in Fort Wayne came to the rescue. Wayne York, a key figure on 765, suggested the 1225 team look into securing grates from Chesapeake & Ohio 2-8-4 No. 2776, displayed in Washington Court House, Ohio. Although 2776 was an Alco product built in 1948, the grates matched those of the Lima engines, evidence of the standardization advanced by the old Advisory Mechanical Committee. Working with York and a sympathetic city councilman, the 1225 team negotiated a long-term loan. Six club members drove down to Washington Court House with a truck and retrieved the 351 castings.

◆　　◆　　◆

By September 1975, everything was in place for a fireup. The club set a target date of Saturday, October 5. Word went out across 1225 Nation, and a number of former members who had graduated made plans to attend. Some of the key old hands from the Pere Marquette—Herschel Christensen, Sam Chidester, and, of course, Pelton—marked their calendars. The current members of the club would be out in force. It promised to be quite a gathering.

Then, just days before the crew was scheduled to light the first fire, there came a sudden setback. MSU's insurer, the Hartford Steam Boiler & Insurance Company, notified the club that it would not provide coverage for the fireup, something the university required. Hartford was willing to sanction 1225 as a stationary boiler because it was not connected to the national railroad system, but only with the certification of the State Boiler Board. But the board had determined that Ken Pelton lacked the necessary credentials. Member Roger Scovill was in the club office when word came, and he said that "it left me feeling very bleak."[3]

The problem involved Pelton's certification as a boiler welder, rather than as a boiler repairman. The latter was the more advanced certification, and the one the state required for certification. Pelton's status as an experienced railroader was enough for federal regulators, but not enough for Michigan. The news was a shock to the club, which had assumed that a "boilermaker" was superior to a "boiler repairman."

Determined to save the October 5 fireup, member Mark Campbell stepped into the fray. A future short-line railroad executive, Campbell was fearless and resourceful. Told that the boiler board would not meet again until later in October, Campbell called its chairman, Bud Vierson, to ask him to expedite the matter. The club was determined to save the October 5 fireup date, and Campbell wouldn't take "no" for an answer.

Vierson was an old hand at boilers; his family's company, Vierson Boiler & Repair of Grand Rapids, has been around since 1936. Perhaps he had some sympathy for these students and their locomotive. Campbell got him to reluctantly agree that, yes, perhaps the board could interview Pelton by telephone to assess his higher-level skills and, yes, perhaps he could poll the board members by phone. Pelton ended up passing his test, and the approval came on Thursday, October 3; the boiler was now a stationary boiler licensed by the state of Michigan, and the university's insurance would cover it. The fireup was back on.

❖   ❖   ❖

Preparations to steam up 1225 moved quickly. The club arranged to retrieve several tons of coal from MSU's Power Plant 65, delivered by pickup truck no less. Scovill scrounged a family-owned portable grain elevator to lift the coal into 1225's tender. It took three days to fill the boiler, once again courtesy of the garden hose strung out to the Landscape Architecture building.

Dawn was three hours away that Saturday when a small crew entered 1225's cab. A pile of scrap wood and waste oil had been thrown onto the coal pile spread across the new grates. At 4 A.M., Sam Williams of Detroit, a retired railroader, longtime member of the venerable Michigan Railroad Club, and a beloved honorary member of the 1225 group, lit a ceremonial fusee and tossed it in the firebox. With that, the thirty-four-year-old locomotive began to get warm again for the first time since 1951.

By 8:30 A.M., 1225 was coming to life, with 100 pounds of steam, enough to start blowing the engine's five-chime Nathan whistle. It wasn't the most melodious of steam locomotive whistles, but its raucous, triumphant sound sent a charge through the gathering crowd. Soon, some astonished and bleary-eyed students from nearby Case Hall came trudging over to the locomotive to ask if the whistling could be toned down. Their request was politely but firmly rejected.

Excitement grew throughout the day. Smoke poured out of 1225's stack, and a southerly wind blew it toward Shaw Lane, blackening one of the old tall pines that since 1957 had stood sentinel by the engine. The whistle continued to wail, audible all the way from Trowbridge junction to Jack Breslin's office in the Administration Building. The boiler eventually reached its operating pressure of 245 psi, setting off safety valves and adding to the general racket. Some scattered applause broke out among the hundreds of people witnessing all the commotion. Inside the cab, one of the water glass tubes exploded with a pop, causing momentary concern. But a calm Christensen told everyone to relax. "Shut her off. They do that often," he said. The crew even fired up the stoker engine.

► Honorary member of the Michigan State University Railroad Club Sam Williams, who once fired locomotives for Seaboard Air Line, shovels coal into 1225's firebox for the first fireup. Photo by John B. Corns.

The fireup lasted deep into the night as the club brought down the fire and allowed the engine to cool. It was as if no one wanted the reverie to end. With the dynamo humming, the locomotive's headlight and running lights cast a warm glow over the work site. Everywhere was the sound of softly hissing steam. The 1225 seemed alive.

The fireup was a success, proving that 1225's thirty-four-year-old boiler was in good shape. But there remained another big step toward making the locomotive operational: repairing and reinstalling all those superheater units, a project that wouldn't be completed until June 10, 1977.

◆　　◆　　◆

The completion of the boiler work was critical for Project 1225. Given the obstacles the group members had overcome in just four years, they would have been entitled to pass out cigars and take a break. But not for long. Any letup could lead to a fatal loss of momentum. Project 1225's support system seemed strong, with hundreds of members contributing dues and donations, but the revenue stream was dependent on a steady dose of incremental

good news. Besides, all they had accomplished so far was to put a stationary boiler back in commission.

The club was coming to grips with a fact of life among student groups everywhere: graduation. One by one, key members of the organization were making the life decisions that come with moving beyond college. Although some were able to begin their careers in the Lansing area, others had to move on. Steve Reeves had long since departed for the air force, and that primal force from the early days, Randy Paquette, was obligated to steer his attention toward a career and a young family. Others drifted off to jobs elsewhere in Michigan and beyond. A headline in the February 1974 newsletter proclaimed "Good luck, Bob," as President Bob Wasko prepared to head home to Cleveland for a job. A year later the newsletter offered similar good wishes

◄ Don Childs (*center*), Pete Camps (*left*), and an unidentified crew member work on fastening the whistle to the steam dome on the eve of the fireup. Photo by John B. Corns.

Light smoke drifts from 1225's stack in the predawn darkness as the October 5, 1975, fireup of the locomotive begins. Photo by Jay Williams.

to Norm Burgess and Phil Atwater, both mainstays on the mechanical crew.

Chuck Julian was especially worried about what might happen to the locomotive. He'd made a considerable commitment to Project 1225 over the years, and failure to finish the job was unthinkable. Although he had graduated in the spring of 1975 with a degree in geology and planned to continue his studies at the University of South Carolina, he decided instead to re-enroll at MSU as a graduate student to keep Project 1225 afloat.

By that point Julian was practically the only student member left. He considered himself the last defense against the locomotive's nemesis in the MSU administration, Jack Breslin, so he scheduled a meeting of the club at which he was the only one present. Julian elected himself president. "I knew that my family would never let me forget that I had worked on a project that failed and the engine was cut up," he said. "But I really became president because of the threat Jack Breslin made, which was that the day the work stopped was the day the torches would come out. I believed him."[4]

► Students and campus visitors gather to witness the fireup as the crew sends a thunderous plume of steam skyward out the 1225's blowdown muffler.
Photo by John B. Corns.

A southerly breeze blows thick coal smoke into an adjacent pine tree during the high point of the fireup. In the background is the Railway Post Office car. Photo by John B. Corns.

The remaining active members of the club—most of them associate members by now—concluded that Project 1225 could continue only if a new organization was formed. It would have to be independent of the university, liberated from the cycle of incoming and outgoing students, run by adults whose lives were more established. The new organization would have to own the locomotive.

◆　◆　◆

Urgency grew with news that the College Spur would be abandoned. With the Shaw Lane power plant long since closed, ending coal deliveries, the only rail traffic MSU saw was an annual delivery of toilet paper in a couple of

▶ The Project 1225 fireup crew poses for a group portrait on Stadium Road as someone in the cab blows the locomotive's whistle. *Front row from left:* Sam Williams, John Titterton, Ken Pelton, Norm Burgess, Jeff Wells, Jim Sneed, two unidentified, John Corns; *Back row from left:* Roger Scovill, Jerry Willson, Craig Riggenberg, Mark Campbell, Pete Camps, Dave Oliver, Aarne Frobom, Herschel Christensen, Kevin Keefe, Sam Chidester, John Hall, unidentified, Bruce Wilmoth, Steve Derocha, Chuck Julian, Bruce Kelly. Photo by John B. Corns.

box cars. The Chesapeake & Ohio, now operating under the name the Chessie System, wanted the spur off its books, and MSU wasn't interested in buying.

In 1979, a group of Project 1225 regulars incorporated the Michigan State Trust for Railway Preservation, Inc., a nonprofit 501(c)(3) organization dedicated to finishing 1225 and running it. With a name obviously tied to its MSU roots, members of the group were determined to retain continuity with the original club, but beyond the name they would be on their own.

Changes at MSU worked in the Trust's favor. With Rollin Baker supporting the new organization, the Trust appealed to the university's new president, Edgar Harden, to acquire 1225. A former MSU professor and more recently president of Northern Michigan University, Harden was a transitional figure who occupied the office for little more than a year after the departure of Clifton R. Wharton in 1978. He met with Julian and agreed to donate 1225 to the Trust if it could demonstrate it was legitimate. It might have helped that Harden had once served as chairman of the Lake Superior & Ishpeming Railroad, based in Marquette.

With 1225's new ownership squared away, the crew arranged to move the engine to a safe stretch of the spur. On a snowy, muddy November 26, 1980, 1225 rolled onto live rails by means of a 275-foot shoofly track constructed by volunteers and a group of Hmong refugees employed by the Julian Foundry. The procedure involved building a new grade from behind the display track, with help from a front-end loader provided by a paving company in Ionia. When the track was in place—once again connecting 1225 to the interstate railroad system—the loader doubled as a locomotive and carefully pulled the engine and Railway Post Office (RPO) farther down the track.

The move off campus was completed the following May when a Chessie System diesel pulled the locomotive and the RPO farther west along the spur to a new location behind an office building on Trowbridge Road on space lent by the Michigan High School Athletic Association. The Trust quickly surrounded the compound with a new chain-link fence, and the restoration got back in business. The biggest job accomplished on Trowbridge was removal of the pony truck so

► Crews have nearly completed installing the new track connecting 1225 with the railroad system. Spartan Stadium is visible in the distance. Photo by Dave Parker, courtesy of Steam Railroading Institute collection.

that its troublesome axle could be turned on a lathe. The rebuilt truck was reinstalled on the engine a few months later.

◆　　◆　　◆

Trowbridge Road could only be a temporary home. The 1225 was parked beside a busy commercial strip, still open to the elements, and there was very little room to work. Nothing further of consequence could be accomplished unless the Trust found a permanent home, a place where the organization could store the locomotive indoors, keep working on it, and, ultimately, have some track to run it.

The MSU Railroad Club had pondered a new location as early as 1976, and after 1979 the Trust stepped up the search in earnest. What emerged in 1982 was the next minor miracle. Over in Owosso, a small city 24 miles northeast of East Lansing, the Trust found a hidden gem: the old locomotive shops of the Ann Arbor Railroad. Largely abandoned but still amazingly well equipped, the ramshackle 1887 brick edifice housed a pair of inspection pits, four 50-ton Whiting column jacks, a 90-inch Niles wheel lathe, a 100-ton

◀ Safe in tow as part of a Grand Trunk Western freight train, 1225 leaves East Lansing and heads for Owosso, crossing the Red Cedar River on February 19, 1983. Photo by Dennis Kennedy, courtesy of *Trains* magazine collection.

Chambersburg press, a Bullard inside/outside-diameter vertical lathe, and various other pieces of antique equipment. It was a nearly complete steam shop. And everything worked! Even if the roof was falling in.

The existence of the shop was a by-product of the April 1, 1976, creation of Conrail, the giant freight railroad formed by the federal government in the wake of the bankruptcies of Penn Central and six other eastern railroads. Conrail's advent meant the likely abandonment of hundreds of miles of Michigan railroads, an economic loss the state had a keen interest in preventing. Taking advantage of Section 402 of the Regional Rail Reorganization Act of 1973, Michigan created a short-line program to acquire much of the threatened track and lease it to designated operators, a template that would become common nationwide in the 1980s.

The state's biggest acquisition was the 300 miles of ex–Ann Arbor track from Toledo northwest to Frankfort via Owosso, Mt. Pleasant, and Cadillac. The historical Ann Arbor Railroad was created in the late nineteenth century to move freight traffic

across the state to Frankfort, thence via carferries across Lake Michigan to four ports in Wisconsin and the Upper Peninsula, bypassing Chicago. Never strong financially, the company was the ward of several railroads, including the Wabash and the Detroit, Toledo & Ironton, until it declared bankruptcy in 1973. After a series of arrangements with other operators, the state in 1983 began leasing the 249 miles of railroad north from Ann Arbor to a new short line called Tuscola & Saginaw Bay (TSBY).

With the state now in the railroad business, it found itself in possession of the engine terminal and yard in Owosso. The TSBY had a base for its diesels there, too, in a separate building. But the old brick pile of a backshop would be good for 1225. Never mind the fact that the old Ann Arbor never fielded a locomotive remotely close to 1225's size. Citing the building's historical value, the Trust

▶ Just in from East Lansing, 1225 has an encounter with a Michigan Interstate GP35 diesel at the steam locomotive's new home in Owosso, February 19, 1983.
Photo by Dennis Kennedy, courtesy of *Trains* magazine collection.

proposed a lease and, with the help of veteran state senator Dominic Jacobetti of Negaunee, secured a rent of only $1 per year.

New digs radically changed the 1225 equation. Suddenly the Trust was a going concern, with a respectable facility to finish what the old student railroad club started. Arrangements were made to move 1225 out of East Lansing. On February 19, 1983, a Grand Trunk Western GP38 diesel coupled to 1225 at Trowbridge and slowly began towing the locomotive and the RPO the 38 miles eastward to the historic junction of Durand. Then a TSBY GP35 took it 11 more miles to the northwest to Owosso.

The ferry move created quite a stir. A large number of railfans were on hand for the departure from East Lansing, and upward of 100 waited for the engine to pass at the stately Durand depot. A long caravan of cars paced the train from East Lansing along M-78 and up M-21 to Owosso. It was a cold, gray day, and 1225 was lifeless. But the locomotive's wheels were moving, there were men in the cab, the bell was ringing, and there was promise in the air.

THE EDITOR ON CAMPUS

By the early spring of 1973, members of the Michigan State University (MSU) Railroad Club were showing some swagger. Whatever the odds still facing Project 1225, they had made impressive strides, and if the locomotive site looked a bit like a junkyard, that was merely the misleading evidence of progress. The crew had already rebuilt a number of key parts. Their new boilermaker, Ken Pelton, was hard at work. The RPO's interior hummed with activity. The club had raised enough money through dues and donations to keep the enterprise moving along.

To celebrate all this effort, the club scheduled a second annual spring banquet. Of course, they needed a good speaker. The number one choice for just about any railroad enthusiast group in America would be the biggest celebrity in the field: David P. Morgan, the veteran editor of *Trains*, the indispensable magazine of the faithful. With characteristic brashness, a banquet committee decided to invite Morgan, with very little expectation he'd say yes.

The timely response from *Trains'* offices in Milwaukee shocked everyone. The editor said he'd be delighted.

Thus, on May 12, 1973, a small contingent of club members drove out to Capitol City Airport to welcome Morgan and his wife, Margaret, arriving in the late morning on a North Central Airlines 580 turboprop. Bemused, perhaps, by his celebrity, Morgan put his nervous hosts at ease as he took a tour of the 1225 site, asking questions here and there about the engine's condition and its resemblance to Nickel Plate 2-8-4s.

The dinner that evening was everything the club wanted it to be. A sold-out crowd jammed a ballroom at East Lansing's Albert Pick Motel, many of them students in not terribly familiar evening wear, as well as a number of railfans from around the Midwest. The throng fell silent when the slight, stooped guest of honor rose to the podium.

Morgan was a great speaker, nearly in spite of himself. Without a scintilla of gesture or flair, and with barely any change in his cadence, the editor simply stared down at his speech and, in his croaky Georgia drawl, delivered a beautifully customized speech. The deadpan delivery was perfect, because it never got in the way of his words.

"We are here to celebrate steam," he said, "and one of the many wonders of steam is its simplicity. Boil water in an enclosed vessel, channel the resultant force against a piston head, then watch and feel as the piston thrusts through the crosshead to main and side rods and driving wheels rotate. No Ph.D., no B.S., no degree or diploma of any kind is necessary to comprehend and be touched by that formula."

His speech touched on the essence of the steam railroad's place in America, invoking some of its greatest names: George and Robert Stephenson, Jay Gould, Abraham Lincoln. For his key theme, he quoted railroading's most flamboyant writer, Lucius Beebe, who described the steam locomotive as "a machine at once useful and beautiful."

Morgan also spoke directly to the club members wearing the scratches and scrapes of their weekend work sessions.

You have picked a machine of good lineage, noble breed. For the Lima Locomotive Works, creator of Pere Marquette 2-8-4 type No. 1225, was surely the scientist of steam. In sophistication of design, in excellence of construction, Lima had no equal among the commercial builders.

So when I first read of the rehabilitation

of Pere Marquette 1225, I was intrigued. . . . For steam locomotives do not belong outdoors behind cyclone fences in parks, jackets rusting, headlight and cab glass broken, gruesome skeletons of the proud, live machines we knew in our youth. Steam locomotives were intended to boil water, produce ton-miles and train-miles, summon young men off the farm.

Morgan's speech climaxed with a stirring promise.

When—I reject the qualifying word "if"—when you have this handsome locomotive in steam, I can assure you that my wife and I will be here. . . . You won't see us. The crowd will be much too large for that. But we will be there. And, just because I have no alma mater, I may just privately adopt Michigan State as my school. For if this university adopts this engine, then this institution will have evidenced itself as truly a place of higher learning, learning not only of the trades, to recall Beebe's words, but learning of the heart.

His closing lines sparked a thunderous ovation.

Alas, Morgan could have not have known that 1225 would run again only after it escaped the MSU campus. Nor would he live long enough to see it in steam. His health began to fail in the late 1980s, and he died in January 1990 at age sixty-two.

Trains magazine editor David P. Morgan, whose speech to the Michigan State University Railroad Club in May 1973 celebrated a machine "at once useful and beautiful." Courtesy of *Trains* magazine collection.

CHAPTER 7

Back on the Main Line

Although the Owosso shop was a godsend, it wasn't like the Michigan State Trust for Railway Preservation could simply move in, turn on the lights, and go to work. Nothing was ever that easy with 1225. In fact, even getting the locomotive into the building was a challenge, due to the poor condition of the tracks leading up to doors of the shop, not to mention the fact that the Ann Arbor Railroad never had a locomotive remotely as large as 1225. The big Berkshire barely fit, even with the tender left outside. With the help of greased rails, a Tuscola & Saginaw Bay (TSBY) diesel operated by a volunteer engineer eased the steam locomotive into its new home on February 19, 1983.

Before the Trust's crew could begin working on the locomotive again, the new tenants had to revive the building and the surrounding infrastructure, a project that required several months. The first order of business was installation of a new spur to the shop and a new switch into the yard. Next came repairs to the shop itself: masonry repairs to the northeast corner of the building, which threatened to cave in, and repairs to the leaky roof and skylight. Workers also updated the electrical service.

As the shop situation gradually improved, work on the locomotive proceeded. The crew might have been pinching themselves, surrounded by all that shop equipment so scarce back at

◄ It was a tight fit for 1225 inside the Owosso shop; the Ann Arbor Railroad never owned anything larger than a 2-8-2. Photo by Jay Williams.

Michigan State University (MSU). Several of the machines came in handy, especially the Bullard lathe for fashioning new piston rings.

The 1225's boiler was ready to go for the most part, thanks to Ken Pelton's work back at MSU, but it still required small repairs, including welding leaks in the two Nicholson thermic syphons in the firebox. A syphon is a narrow, funnel-shaped steel fabrication that circulates water through the middle of the firebox, connecting the bottom of the boiler with the top of the firebox. A secondary function is to support the firebrick arch. Its main advantage was to increase efficiency by modulating the temperature of the water across the breadth of the firebox. Subject to incredible stress, the syphons could be a weak link in the whole boiler system.

The Owosso team must have done good work, because they passed the biggest test of all on September 5, 1985, when a Federal Railroad Administration (FRA) boiler inspector visited 1225 to inspect it and write up a critique. Other than calling for a few additional minor repairs, he liked what he saw: the Trust won a one-year extended certification of the boiler tubes. Now, 1225 could operate under its own power.

◆ ◆ ◆

The headline in the Winter 1986 issue of *Project 1225* carried the all-capital-letters headline everyone had been waiting for: "SHE MOVED." The newsletter chronicled the events of November 30, 1985, when the crew fired up the locomotive and operated it short distances outside the shop. The session lasted only a few minutes and did not involve the locomotive's operating systems beyond the boiler and running gear. But it was a huge boost for the Trust. The engine had run under its own power for the first time since 1951. It had put the lie to that old club slogan, "It'll never run."

Subsequent fireups in August 1986 and June 1987 also were successful, allowing the crew to test a number of accessories, including the air compressors, inspirator, stoker, generator, and feedwater system. Many of these were parts restored years earlier by the students at MSU. The general reaction of the crew was aptly described by Rod Crawford, who had become the Trust's

▶ Track leading into the Owosso shop building had to be repaired before the huge Berkshire could be carefully moved inside. Courtesy of Steam Railroading Institute collection.

chief mechanical officer: "We have come a long way from November 1985, when we fired it up, moved it 50 feet and back, dumped the fire and were greatly relieved that the whole darned thing did not melt in front of our eyes."[1]

Crawford's relief was well earned. A career mechanical engineer with the Ford Motor Company, he had retired from the automaker and began devoting a substantial amount of his time to Project 1225. He also brought a set of technology skills unknown to the old heads back in Wyoming. One of his innovations was the use of computer-aided design (CAD) for various projects on the locomotive, including the fabrication of a new boiler jacket. Crawford loaded original boiler drawings and other original documents into his CAD software to create a set of full-size paper patterns that could be used to cut the sheet metal for the jacket. By the fall of 1987, 1225 was completely rejacketed, with a fit and finish the builders at Lima would have admired.

◆   ◆   ◆

By the summer of 1988, 1225 was ready to roll. The only question was where. The

TSBY was the obvious place to do it, and the railroad's president, Larry Judd, had been accommodating to his fellow tenants at the Owosso shops. But Judd was reluctant to run 1225 on his main line out of concern for how it might affect his freight trains. He did, however, offer an alternative: the lightly used Chesaning Branch.

Formerly part of the New York Central's (NYC's) line from Lansing to Saginaw, the TSBY branch linked Owosso with Chesaning and St. Charles, two small towns to the northeast. It would give 1225 a flat, forgiving 22-mile stretch to stretch its legs. But the track was a problem. The branch's 106-pound rail had supported NYC 4-8-2s, which were nearly as large as 1225, but far too many of the wooden ties had deteriorated. Members of the Trust were obliged to scrounge 1,100 surplus ties and install them themselves, with the help of a Shiawassee County judge who conscripted several nonviolent inmates under the heading of community service.

The big moment came Labor Day weekend, as 1225 successfully made several trips over three days running light over the

Chesaning Branch. The locomotive sprang a leak in one of its superheater tubes on the second day, so the engine was towed back to Owosso for a quick overnight repair, then was cut loose again the following day, September 5, Labor Day. This time 1225 performed flawlessly, once with TSBY's Judd at the throttle. "She responds nicely," he said.

The successful trial runs allowed the Trust to go ahead with its first weekend of public excursions, October 8 and 9. The trips were operated under the auspices of the Shiawassee Valley Railroad, a nonprofit operating entity set up by the Trust and communities along the route. The new railroad gave the parties a vehicle for making additional improvements to the Chesaning Branch and shielded the Trust from liability. As Aarne Frobom stated, "[It's] basically a tourist railroad that only comes into existence three or four times a year, with hired cars and a locomotive that's a bit too large for the job."[2]

More than 2,300 passengers showed up to ride the Shiawassee Valley, and they got their money's worth. Operating as a revenue-producing asset for the first time since 1951, 1225 put on a great show, smoking up a storm, whistling across the soybean- and cornfields, drawing big crowds at every grade crossing. In St. Charles, officials broke a bottle of champagne on 1225's pilot beam and gave the crew a key to the village.

Held to a demure 25 miles per hour and accompanied by a TSBY diesel at the end of the train (with nowhere to turn, the train had to operate bidirectionally), the excursions only hinted at the potential of the Trust's Super Power locomotive. But the performance was enough to lift the spirits of the long-suffering mechanical crew. On that Saturday night, camped beside the warm, simmering engine, a large contingent of former MSU Railroad Club members joined the new crew in an evening of toasts and high fives.

◆　　◆　　◆

As satisfying as the Owosso trips were for the 1225 team, everyone yearned for a chance to see the locomotive perform on a main-line railroad. The Trust finally got its chance due to the efforts of the C. P. Huntington Chapter of the National Railway Historical Society (NRHS),

◀ In a view from atop the Owosso shop, onlookers gather to watch the August 2, 1986, fireup of 1225. Photo by Jay Williams.

based in Huntington, West Virginia, and chosen to host the 1991 NRHS national convention. In those days, NRHS conventions were generally a three- or four-day bash featuring main-line excursions, preferably behind steam. For 1991, C. P. Huntington was dreaming big, hatching a plan that involved trips using both 1225 and the Nickel Plate (NKP) No. 765 in Fort Wayne. The chapter had the blessing of CSX Transportation, which in 1986 had become the successor company to the Chessie System.

Seen in the context of today's railroad environment, the Huntington project seems almost impossible. Most big freight railroads keep steam at arm's length, and since 2000 CSX has wanted no part of historic railroading. But railroad managements can be fickle, and in the early 1990s steam operators enjoyed a brief honeymoon with CSX management. Much of this was due to Richard Young, the railroad's vice president of passenger service. Young's job was ostensibly to manage the freight carrier's relationships with Amtrak and various commuter agencies. But Young had a soft spot for steam, as well as the ear of CSX president Jerry R. Davis, himself a railfan-friendly presence at CSX's Jacksonville headquarters.

But first things first. The railroad would have to have 100 percent confidence in any steam locomotive invited to Huntington. One of the scheduled engines, 765, already had operated a number of successful main-line trips since its return to service in 1980. Most were in the Midwest, but the NKP 2-8-4 also had traveled several hundred miles east to New Jersey and back for trips during the 1988 NRHS convention, as well as across Norfolk Southern through parts of Kentucky, Tennessee, Alabama, Georgia, and North Carolina. The Fort Wayne group and its machine were nothing if not seasoned.

The 1225, on the other hand, had been restricted to the slow speeds and light loads on the TSBY, which was, after all, a short line. The engine and its crew had performed effectively, but 1225 was a main-line thoroughbred, and, for anything on the TSBY, it was overqualified. Young required that 1225 prove itself in a tougher environment and decided to allow the locomotive to haul a CSX freight train.

▶ Heading west with a twenty-three-car freight train, 1225 rolls along the former Pere Marquette main line near Williamston on October 20, 1990. Photo by Kevin P. Keefe.

What followed on Saturday and Sunday, October 20 and 21, 1990, was magical, as 1225 returned to its home rails for a 262-mile round trip over the original Pere Marquette (PM) between Plymouth and Grand Rapids, including an overnight service stay at the Wyoming shops. On Friday night, the TSBY included 1225 in its regular train to Ann Arbor and dropped off the locomotive at a place called Annpere, the Ann Arbor Railroad's junction with the PM near Howell. Early the next morning the engine proceeded east to Plymouth yard, where the locomotive was turned and then coupled onto a westbound train of twenty-three freight cars and a caboose.

The CSX's official switch list that day accounted for 1,265 tons spread across eleven loads and twelve empties, an easy train for 1225. And the Berkshire was on its own; CSX decided it wasn't necessary to include a diesel helper. CSX's written orders to the non-steam-era pilot crew simply referred to their train's assigned power as "Lead Unit: No. PM 1225."

A throng of railfans from across the

country and dozens of members of the Trust showed up that golden afternoon to chase 1225 across the PM's old Grand Rapids Division. They were in for a treat. After departing Plymouth at 3 P.M., 1225 and its train moved smartly across the railroad, covering the first leg to East Lansing in less than two hours, highlighted by a big crowd at Trowbridge, just southwest of the MSU campus. If you had been standing at 1225's old site on Stadium Road, you easily could have heard the whistle.

After weaving slowly through Lansing, the train stopped for water at CSX's Ensel yard on the northwest side of the city. A huge crowd watched the procedure. Soon 1225 galloped off again, put on a noisy show on a graceful S-curve and high bridge over the Grand River at Grand Ledge, then vaulted off toward the setting sun at speeds approaching 60 miles per hour through the flat country surrounding

◄ The 1225 freight extra rolls past a factory in Lansing on the westbound leg of its October 20, 1990, trip to the Wyoming shops. Photo by Victor Hand.

Sunfield, Lake Odessa, and on toward Grand Rapids. Drivers pacing the train on State Highway 43 had a difficult time keeping up.

The locomotive finally arrived at Wyoming for its overnight stop and was parked in the shadow of the huge old PM shop buildings. No one missed the fact that the last time this happened was in 1957, just before the locomotive was sent to MSU. Although the roundhouse and turntable were gone, the old coaling tower still stood, and 1225 parked beside it, setting a romantic scene for a few crew and photographers who lingered in the heat of the boiler, trading stories into the night.

The following morning brought clouds and rain. The crew had to top off 1225's water tank with several garden hoses, proving that Wyoming wasn't the place it used to be. By 10:20 A.M. the engine was ready to go to work again, hauling an eastbound train of twelve loads and twelve empties, or 1,747 tons. This time the train encountered several delays, mostly to take siding for various other CSX freights, but also to stop to remove a hobo before the train was even out of Grand Rapids. The test run came to an end late Sunday night when the freight cars were set off at Annpere and a TSBY diesel piloted the steam locomotive back to Owosso.

The freight run across mid-Michigan was galvanizing for the Trust. The emotional satisfaction of putting 1225 to work on the PM surpassed even the crew's most optimistic expectations. More important, the organization proved to CSX that its Lima 2-8-4, properly maintained and operated, was as capable of working on the modern railroad as NKP 765. With that, CSX was ready to make the commitment. The 1225 would go to Huntington.

◆　◆　◆

The 1225's trip to West Virginia gave the engine an opportunity to perform on a national stage. In 1991, the NRHS still was thriving as the country's largest organization of railroad enthusiasts, with a membership near 20,000. A good convention with good trips might draw nearly 2,000 attendees. The engines were the stars, and Huntington would feature three: Pere Marquette 1225, Nickel Plate 765, and also Norfolk & Western 2-6-6-4 No. 1218, an articulated thoroughbred that

▶ The 1225 roars through Alto, Michigan, on the October 21, 1990, return leg of its round-trip freight run on CSX to Grand Rapids. Photo by Victor Hand.

at the time was one of the stars of the Norfolk Southern steam program.

At many NRHS gatherings, the ferry moves to get various steam engines to the convention site were as interesting as the convention excursions themselves, sometimes more so. For Huntington, CSX came up with a winner. First came 1225's run to Plymouth on August 3, where the engine picked up a twenty-five-car freight train and the private car *Indianapolis*, loaned by attorney Dave McClure for the use of 1225's crew. The route southward would take the engine along CSX's former Baltimore & Ohio (B&O) through Toledo to North Lima, Ohio, where it would meet 765. Then, together, the two Berkshires would head south past the old Lima Locomotive Works plant, stop for service in Dayton, and proceed to CSX's Queensgate Yard in Cincinnati. On the second day the engines would follow the old Chesapeake & Ohio (C&O) Ohio River main line to Huntington.

The ferry trip was memorable on a number of counts. The departure from Plymouth got off to a fitful start when the

requisite FRA inspector showed up and determined 1225 would have to be limited to 20 miles per hour. The engine didn't have a speedometer. In fact, in steam days, steam locomotives often lacked speedometers, and FRA rules did not require them. But this particular inspector didn't understand the steam part of the rules, so the 2-8-4 took it slow as far as Toledo, where CSX added a diesel to provide the speedometer.

Expectations were heightened at North Lima in the late afternoon when 1225 and its train coasted into the old B&O yard, where a large crowd had gathered to witness the first encounter of the two Advisory Mechanical Committee–design 2-8-4s. After some switching—and much friendly whistling—the locomotives doubleheaded southbound, 765 in the lead. Within minutes came one of the emotional highs of the journey as the two engines steamed slowly past the abandoned Lima works. Amid a sudden thunderstorm, the engines' whistles and exhausts ricocheted off the brick walls of the buildings that turned out both machines a half-century earlier.

Later, the Trust's Rod Crawford reflected on the reunion at Lima: "What I saw . . . was very emotional. One of my biggest dreams had been just to get 765 and 1225 together in the same yard. The doubleheader was frosting on the cake."[3]

The rest of the ferry trip went smoothly. The steam crews made a bleary-eyed arrival at Queensgate about 4 A.M., then departed just six hours later for Huntington. The two Berkshires made a fine sight that Saturday, speeding eastbound along the Ohio River down the graceful C&O double-track tangents, leaving behind most of the train-chasers on clogged Kentucky Highway 8 and U.S. 23. The ferry train paused for servicing at the historic C&O engine terminal at Russell, Kentucky, and arrived at Huntington in the late afternoon. Both were parked for the rest of the week at the imposing downtown depot, still used by CSX as division offices.

The following Friday, August 9, arrived amid great expectations. On the program was a side-by-side performance of both Berkshires. The excursion was inspired by a similar stunt staged in 1987 by Norfolk Southern (NS) in Roanoke, Virginia, involving NS's two Norfolk & Western

◀ With 765 in the lead, doubleheaded Berkshires wait in a siding for a meet with a CSX freight at Botkins, Ohio, as the steam locomotives head southward for Huntington, West Virginia, on August 3, 1991. Photo by Victor Hand.

engines, 1218 and 4-8-4 No. 611, the famous streamlined "J." That convention, sponsored by the Roanoke Chapter, NRHS, was fresh in everyone's memory. What didn't need to be explained was the rivalry between NS and CSX, or even between the Roanoke and Huntington NRHS chapters for that matter.

Huntington's "dueling engines" would begin with a 38-mile eastbound trip from Huntington to the small town of St. Albans. The thirty-one-car excursion train was assigned to 1225; 765 would haul twenty brand-new coal gondolas, fresh from CSX's Raceland (Kentucky) car shops. Departing simultaneously in the morning, the Berkshires paced each other down the double-track, alternately pulling ahead or falling behind each other, delighting the hundreds of passengers riding behind 1225.

The highlight of the day came in the hamlet of Hurricane, population 6,200, a town split down the middle by the CSX main line in a deep cut. The town got its name from nearby Hurricane Creek, discovered in the late 1700s by surveyors who came upon a vast forest laid flat, apparently by a violent windstorm. On this Saturday in 1991, the name would prove to be apt.

The gently sloping sides of the cut made a natural amphitheater. Soon after the two trains stopped, the hillsides and a street bridge filled up with hundreds of photographers disgorged from the excursion train. The locomotives and their trains then backed up some distance before charging back again a few minutes later, side by side in perfect tandem, whistles screaming and exhausts barking. Hurricane literally roared, and applause broke out from the crowd as coal smoke drifted down over their heads.

After the run by, the doubleheaded engines headed back from St. Albans amid a memorable thunderstorm. It was a fitting end to an exciting day. Most witnesses at Hurricane who had been at Roanoke in 1987 agreed: the side-by-side romp of 1225 and 765 was every bit as exciting as the Norfolk Southern show. Perhaps the most excited was a smiling Joe Sigafoose, engineer of 1225, whose day job was running trains for TSBY. Thousands of frames of film caught Sigafoose's green-and-white polka dot Kromer cap in the window of 1225's cab.

▶ The two Berkshires race each other down the CSX main line approaching Hurricane, West Virginia, on August 9, 1991. Photo by Victor Hand.

There was more in store on Saturday: a 148-mile run to Hinton, West Virginia, and back with doubleheaded 2-8-4s. The long day would take the train across the heart of the C&O's fabled West Virginia main line, including 52 winding miles through the wild New River national park. The route included such storied C&O locations as Gauley Bridge, Hawk's Nest, Thurmond, Prince, and Hinton. The trip also would cover each side of the C&O's unusual 11-mile split main line on both sides of the river between Hawk's Nest and Sewell.

The trip shouldn't have been difficult. With only about 2,500 tons of train, the two engines would have an easy time with grades that did not exceed 0.48 percent. The outbound trip went smoothly until a service stop at Montgomery, east of Charleston, where it was discovered that 1225 had developed a small steam leak in one of the thermic syphons. The leak itself wasn't catastrophic; the 1225 crew later determined that a repair made in 1951 in the engine's last months had failed. But the 1225 crew decided to reduce steam pressure for the rest of the trip, leaving the work of hauling the train to 765. The leak and delays associated with servicing the engines caused the excursion to return to Huntington in darkness, several hours late.

◆　　◆　　◆

The 1225 needed a temporary repair of the left-side syphon before it could head back to Michigan, so the return ferry trip was delayed a couple of days. The engine needed to cool down enough to allow a CSX boiler repairman from Huntington to climb into the firebox and weld the crack on the syphon. The following Wednesday, 1225 made a memorable run back toward Owosso, covering the nearly

◀ Crowds of excursion passengers and townspeople gather in Hurricane, West Virginia, to witness Nickel Plate 765 (*left*) and Pere Marquette 1225 in their side-by-side run. Photo by John B. Corns.

250 miles from Russell to Toledo in about twelve hours, all with Joe Sigafoose at the throttle. The engine even hauled another freight train, twenty-one cars, north from Russell at speeds approaching 60 miles per hour.

From the perspective of more than twenty years, the Huntington trip can be seen as a triumph for 1225, even though the leaky syphon dampened the engine's performance. Certainly it was wonderful railroad theater, with 1225 matching up with another Van Sweringen 2-8-4 to demonstrate Will Woodard's Super Power theories all over again. And do some of it in the shadow of the Lima Locomotive Works.

CSX and 765 officials came away with a positive impression. Fort Wayne's Rich Melvin, one of 765's regular engineers, praised the 1225 crew. "For the first time out, they did a fine job. They can be very proud of themselves."[4] And CSX's Young was relieved: "From our perspective, this went very well. I didn't hear any unfavorable comments from anyone."[5]

But 1225 had a serious problem. The syphons would need to be replaced. Both were beyond their service lives. Replacing them would be complicated and expensive. The Owosso shop didn't have the capability to bend $5/16$-inch boiler plate into the convoluted shape of the syphon. The crew wasn't even sure how to get the old syphons out of the firebox. Moreover, a number of staybolts had begun to fail, leading to questions about the side sheets in the firebox. Back in Owosso, just weeks removed from their bravura performance at Hurricane, a disappointed Trust reluctantly canceled the rest of steam operations for 1991. Once again, they'd have to dig deep.

▶ Tandem Berkshires impress the crowd in a photo run-by at Thurmond, West Virginia, during the August 10, 1991, doubleheader. Photo by Kevin P. Keefe.

AT HOME IN OWOSSO

Of all the good fortune that befell Project 1225 over the years, none was more welcomed than the emergence of Owosso as a base of operations. To find a functional, reasonably well-equipped shop complex only 40 miles from East Lansing was ridiculously good luck. To get it at such a reasonable price was a minor miracle. And to share it with a sympathetic freight railroad only made the arrangement sweeter.

And yet, from a historical perspective, Owosso's old Ann Arbor Railroad (AA) shops are antithetical to 1225. The engine crews of the Pere Marquette's Berkshires were used to romping up and down a splendid right-of-way at speeds of 60 miles per hour, sharing the railroad with passenger trains that were doing 79 miles per hour. They ended their runs at sprawling terminals equipped with huge roundhouses and concrete coaling towers in Detroit, Grand Rapids, and Chicago. Almost everything about the Pere Marquette was major league.

Owosso, by contrast, was a sleepy place. Tucked inside a residential neighborhood on the east side of town, the AA terminal operated at a slow pace, catering to a modest collection of small steam locomotives. In its mid-twentieth-century heyday, when it was under the control of the Wabash, the AA ran its freight trains with a motley assortment of Alco 2-8-0s and 2-8-2s, and, at the top of the roster, a quartet of Baldwin-built 2-10-2s. These Santa Fe–type engines were big for the railroad, though, and held to 30 miles per hour on account of the AA's modest track. In 1942, the railroad got rid of the 2-10-2s, selling them to Kansas City Southern, where they presumably reached more of their potential.

Like the Pere Marquette, though, the AA successfully matched its motive power to its business needs, and small Consolidations and Mikados were all that was required for the slow trains that trekked northwestly across the state to serve the railroad's principal business of bridge traffic over Lake Michigan via carferries. First organized in 1878 by business interests based in the city of Ann Arbor, the Toledo, Ann Arbor & North Michigan reached its port at Elberta, adjacent to Frankfort, in 1883. Soon it was delivering cars across the water to Manitowoc and Kewaunee, Wisconsin, and Menominee and Manistique, Michigan, in the Upper Peninsula.

By going all in on bridge traffic with a single main line, the railroad's builders managed to miss every important industry city in the state. Thus there was comparatively little on-line business, which contributed to the railroad falling into receivership from 1931 to 1942. In fact, the historian Robert I. Warrick has noted that the AA "was a steamship line as much as it was a railroad." By 1940, the railroad's 320 water miles eclipsed its 292 land miles, and freight train schedules were tied closely to sailing times in Elberta.[6]

Ironically, the AA had something in common with the Pere Marquette (or at least with its successor, the Chesapeake & Ohio): it got rid of steam early. By the end of 1951, all AA steam service had ended, giving way to what became a conspicuous fleet of Alco diesels. The Wabash equipped its ward with S1 and S2 switchers, a quartet of RS2 road switchers, and, most famously, a set of six FA-2 cab diesels done up in a Wabash-style "follow-the-flag" paint scheme. Throughout the late 1950s and into the 1960s, photographers were drawn to Owosso by the promise of getting a chance to shoot the FAs.

The AA took another major turn in 1961 when it was acquired by the Detroit, Toledo & Ironton (DT&I). The DT&I had some successful years with the AA, but by the mid-1970s the old short line's fortunes had dwindled, and in the 1980s the entire railroad north of Ann Arbor metamorphosed into the Tuscola & Saginaw Bay and later the Great Lakes Central, operating via contract on state-owned track.

Fortunately for the operators of 1225, the state of Michigan has continued to pour millions of dollars into the former AA right-of-way. The expenditures are made in the name of freight service, notably the heavy-duty trains that bring sand out of the huge pits at Yuma, northwest of Cadillac. But the good track also has proved to be a windfall for the big Berkshire, which, in an earlier season, would have had no business running on the old AA.

▶ A pair of Alco FA-2 diesels in the Ann Arbor Railroad shops at Owosso, Michigan, in November 1963. Photo by Roger Meade, courtesy of *Trains* magazine collection.

CHAPTER 8

THE CHRISTMAS LOCOMOTIVE

Ever since regular-service main-line steam disappeared around 1960, the hardy souls who keep the technology alive have had to scrounge from time to time. No one makes the necessary parts anymore. The network of companies that manufactured injectors, staybolts, low-water alarms, cross-compound air pumps, and the like is gone, save for a handful of boutique artisans who serve the tourist railroad industry. If you need a part, you'll likely have to bum it off someone else's display engine. Or make it from scratch yourself.

That was the dilemma facing the 1225 crew once the engine was parked back in the Owosso shop after the trip to Huntington. Although 1225 could feasibly operate without the syphons in the light-duty environment of the Tuscola & Saginaw Bay (TSBY), there was never any question about replacing them. The Michigan State Trust for Railway Preservation, after all, was a preservation organization. Running a Lima Super Power locomotive without tapping the full power of that boiler would be heresy.

But the only way to fix the problem was to fabricate entirely new syphons, a daunting task. The syphons are not separate, discrete appurtenances that are simply bolted on the engine. They are integral to the firebox and thus to 1225's entire ability to develop steam. In the years since the steam era, syphon repairs were rare.

◀ The 1225 kicks up snow on a February 2008 freight-train photo charter north of Owosso. The locomotive's headlight is off in the custom of 1940s-era daytime operation. Photo by Victor Hand.

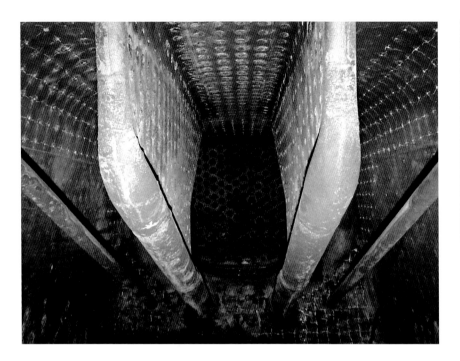

▲ Interior view of 1225's smokebox shows its two thermic syphons, suspended from the crown sheet of the firebox. Courtesy of Steam Railroading Institute collection.

◀ Custom-made steel mandrels gave the crew a form over which syphon sheets could be formed by hand, with a mallet. Courtesy of Steam Railroading Institute collection.

Undaunted, the Owosso crew decided to give it a go. The team spent much of 1992 designing not only the new syphon parts but also the tools and method of manufacture. The cost of the entire repair was estimated at $18,000, but the Trust got a boost late in the year when it won a $7,800 preservation grant from the Potomac Chapter of the National Railway Historical Society (NRHS). Matching revenue and gifts from Trust members made up the rest.

The project required the services of several local companies. Patterns for the new tools were made by member Jerry Dosh, using a computer-controlled milling machine that incorporated computer-aided design (CAD) drawings developed by Rod Crawford from 1225's original blueprints. Astech Foundry of Vassar, Michigan, made castings for the steel mandrels, which basically are solid forms over which the boiler repairmen would hammer the steel sheet. Providing its service gratis, Simplicity Engineering of Durand used a numeric-control torch to cut the sheets into the correct patterns. Some of these pieces were rolled and bent cold into the correct shapes by Aluminum & Architectural Metals Company of Detroit.

Then it was time for old-fashioned handwork. Each piece of sheet was heated to the correct temperature, put in place around the mandrels, and hammered into shape with wooden mallets. Beating the steel sheets and reheating them with acetylene torches took about two hours for each of the six pieces. It was arduous. As Aarne Frobom explained in the Trust's newsletter, "Most of our regular volunteer crew and a few visitors took a hand at the mallets, partly for the experience but mostly because it wore people out in a hurry." Even the hammers were homemade, created by mechanic Mark Holton using ironwood trees found around Shiawassee County.

The nearly finished hammered parts then were carefully cut to the precision sizes required for the firebox by welder Jeff Flisnik of the Purvis & Foster Company of Detroit, heat treated, and installed in the firebox over several weeks. The crew also had to install more than 100 staybolts inside the syphons, a tricky business that required several more weeks. The finishing touch was the installation of new arch tubes across the firebox, between the syphons, used to support the archbrick.

Looking back, Frobom marvels at the ingenuity of the Trust's mechanical department. "The cool thing about the syphons was the extent to which it forced us to rediscover original techniques, because nothing else would work. Because we could not stamp out a new syphon in one piece, nor get it into the firebox, we replicated the approach the railroads used."[1]

◆　◆　◆

Completion of the syphons allowed the Trust to put 1225 back in service around Owosso, including using it for a novel fund-raising program called "Engineer for an Hour." Begun in September 1993 and repeated at various intervals since, it gave anyone willing to spend the $400 fee an opportunity to run 1225 over a short stretch of track south of Henderson, five miles north of Owosso, under the watchful eye of the regular crew. Among the sixty-seven people who signed up for the program in August 1996 was Randy Paquette of Otisville. The former Michigan

State University (MSU) Railroad Club mechanical guru finally had a chance to fulfill a dream that went back more than a quarter-century. Former club member Steve Derocha spent an afternoon quietly watching from a lawn chair, before passing away several months later. And MSU machinist Don Childs had a turn at the throttle, too. It was fantasy fulfillment, and for the locomotive, it was lucrative.

Good thing, because even with a pair of brand-new syphons, 1225's boiler would soon require another makeover. The reflueing performed by Ken Pelton way back in 1974 and 1975 had run its course. The Federal Railroad Administration (FRA) had granted various certification extensions over the years, allowing the Trust to keep operating in its first few years of excursion service, but as 1995 arrived the agency needed to inspect the inside of the boiler again.

Once again, the laborious project required the removal of all 275 tubes and flues, to be remaindered for scrap, and the installation of 275 new ones. The Trust counted 1,650 various operations involved in the job. With the tubes removed, an inspection revealed that 1225's boiler was still in excellent condition. Some cracks were found around some staybolts at the bottom of the combustion chamber by the rear tube sheet, but they were easily repaired. The enterprising Trust managed to do the entire project for an astoundingly low $40,000.

One reward for all the hard work came in March 1995 when the locomotive earned a listing on the National Register of Historic Places, a program of the National Park Service. In citing 1225, the Register nomination noted the engine "embodies the characteristics of the last and most powerful steam locomotives." While the listing carried no guarantees of funding or continued preservation, it underscored the Trust's mission to use the machine to teach something about history.

◆   ◆   ◆

Repairs to the firebox and installation of new tubes brought hopes of another major cross-country trip, this time to the grand opening of the Steamtown National Historic Site in Scranton, Pennsylvania, in July 1995. Steamtown had moved to Scranton from Vermont in 1984, became a

◄ The Detroit River tunnel was too tight for 1225, but not for this quartet of Alco diesels emerging from the tunnel on the Canadian side with an eastbound New York Central train in March 1964. Photo by Roger Meade, courtesy of *Trains* magazine collection.

National Historic Site in 1986, and in 1995 was poised to become part of the National Parks Service after $80 million in renovations. The huge celebration would include Milwaukee Road No. 261, a 4-8-4 built in 1944 by Alco and operated out of Minneapolis by North Star Rail, which leased the locomotive from the National Railroad Museum in Green Bay, Wisconsin. The Steamtown celebration promised to be historic, and everyone wanted 1225 to join the party.

For a while, Scranton looked like a wonderful opportunity for 1225. The locomotive's latest renovations were complete, and the Berkshire gleamed in its new jacket and paint job. The Trust secured a $2,000 gift from *Trains* magazine to help pay for coal for the trip. Working with Steamtown, the Trust made plans to run the engine from Detroit to Buffalo via the Canadian Pacific (CP) through Ontario, then on to Scranton over the former Lackawanna main line via Binghamton, New York.

On June 19, only a few days before 1225 was due to leave for Scranton, a team of clearance engineers from the CP showed up at Owosso and determined that 1225 would not fit through the CP's tunnel under the Detroit River because it was too wide at the cylinders. The same determination was made for 261, already on its way from Minneapolis. CSX hastily made plans to reroute both engines to Buffalo through Ohio on its former Baltimore & Ohio main line. However, 1225's trip was canceled with just two days to spare when organizers in Scranton declined to boost the Trust's compensation for the extra 500 miles 1225 would travel through Ohio and Pennsylvania.

▶ Resplendent in a refurbished jacket and rebuilt boiler, 1225 was in peak condition at the moment the Scranton trip was scrubbed. Courtesy of Steam Railroading Institute collection.

Although the Trust drew criticism from some quarters, it maintained a tough line on charging for 1225, and its fees were based on hard lessons learned. Perhaps more than any other main-line steam operator, the Trust had taken a sharp pencil to its operating costs to determine how much it really took to run the locomotive. Back in 1991, after 1225 returned from Huntington, Rod Crawford made a series of calculations that blended direct and indirect boiler, running-gear, coal, and water-treatment costs. He came up with $3,400 per day. Based on that figure, looking back the Trust figured it actually lost money on the original Shiawassee Valley excursions as well as the safari to Huntington. It wasn't going to let that happen at Steamtown, regardless of the public exposure.

As usual, Aarne Frobom put the Trust's policy in perspective: "We were faced with the unenviable choice of operating the engine without compensation, versus losing the chance to exhibit it in a prestigious showcase. We made a very firm promise to ourselves some time back to avoid operating the engine at a loss. While we might set this policy aside for good reason from time to time, we were not prepared to abandon it on a few hours' notice, for an operation that would be planned as it went."[2]

◆　　◆　　◆

The collapse of the Steamtown trip was a keen disappointment to everyone involved with 1225, but the Trust couldn't waste a lot of time ruminating about it. In truth, the party in Scranton would have been a bit of a sideshow, distracting the organization from the main business at hand, which was to make a long-term commitment either to Owosso or to somewhere else.

Although the Trust enjoyed a good relationship with its landlord, the TSBY, the organization had the uncertain status of a tenant, a situation that didn't square with the Trust's dreams of creating a substantial museum of steam railroad technology. One thing was for certain: the rickety old Ann Arbor engine house was reaching the end of its economically viable life.

The Trust hired architects to draw up plans for a lavish facility that included a combined four-stall roundhouse and exhibit hall, a machine shop for heavy repairs, a turntable and water plug, a crew quarters, and various other features. It was a big dream, too big for Owosso. So the organization looked elsewhere, inspecting locations around the state that might work. It found a large roundhouse and turntable on private property in Niles. It looked at the old Pere Marquette engine terminal in Saginaw, still a part of CSX, and found other possible sites in Durand, Flint, Holland, and Plymouth.

While all this was happening, some soul-searching in the organization led to discussions of adopting a new, more focused brand name. The Trust had evolved beyond its almost total orientation toward 1225, picking up various pieces of other railroad equipment for its collection, including a Pere Marquette caboose, two Ann Arbor cabooses, and the Chesapeake & Ohio 10-6 Pullman sleeper *City of Ashland*, and it leased a spiffy little 0-4-0T tank engine, Flagg Coal Company No. 75, in perfect operating condition. In January 2000, the Trust announced it would operate under a new name, the Steam Railroading Institute (SRI).

The SRI's first big acquisition was

▲ Dennis Braid (*center*) and Rod Crawford (*right*) watch as a member of the mechanical crew hammers into shape a new syphon, wrapped tightly around a mandrel. Courtesy of Steam Railroading Institute collection.

significant: a 100-foot turntable from, of all places, New Buffalo, where 1225 had sat derelict in the mid-1950s. Built by the American Bridge Company in 1919, the original turntable was 90 feet long, barely able to accommodate Pere Marquette's 2-8-4s. The SRI had the turntable transported to Owosso and began structural repairs, and later lengthened it.

In the end, the SRI determined its handsome new turntable would stay in Owosso. The other potential museum sites had turned out to be problematic, due to redevelopment costs, but mostly because of difficulties finding a friendly railroad connection. In the end, the organization concluded that there was no place like home. On January 22, 2003, the SRI's new executive director, Dennis Braid, the Trust's first full-time paid employee, sat down with TSBY chairman and CEO Jim Shepherd and bought 3.55 acres from the railroad for $71,000.

Without an open-minded host railroad, a large locomotive isn't going anywhere. For the Milwaukee Road 261 group in Minneapolis, it has meant carefully cultivating good relations with the CP and Burlington Northern Santa Fe. For the Nickel Plate 765 in Fort Wayne, it has been Norfolk Southern. Fortunately, for the SRI, enlightened management shared the very same property. "The thing that kept us in Owosso was the attitude of the TSBY management," explains Aarne Frobom. "Before Jim Shepherd came along, we didn't know if we'd be thrown out, so we went looking statewide. Of course, it is the trackage rights on the former Ann Arbor that is the main location factor."

◆   ◆   ◆

Even if 1225 never did anything beyond pulling excursions out of Owosso, its presence on the railroad in 2002 as a living, breathing machine was reason enough to celebrate. The locomotive was in safe hands in the Owosso shop. It had exceeded its original Pere Marquette service life by several decades. It had become one of the most-watched large steam locomotives in America, entertaining thousands of passengers and trackside admirers with excursions on the Shiawassee Valley.

But that was nothing compared to the audience that would see it after Dennis Braid picked

The party 1225 missed: Milwaukee Road 4-8-4 261 attracts a throng around the turntable during the June 1995 opening of the Steamtown National Historic Site in Scranton, Pennsylvania. Photo by Bruce Kelly, courtesy of *Trains* magazine collection.

up the phone one day in April of that year. The call was from Hollywood. A researcher from Castle Rock Entertainment had some interesting questions about 1225—questions pertaining to a new movie called *The Polar Express*.

Anyone familiar with children's literature already knew about *The Polar Express*, the best-selling 1985 book by Grand Rapids native Chris Van Allsburg. With its sweet, life-affirming story about a boy's faith in good things and its distinctive, vivid illustrations of the mythic steam train that carried him away to the North Pole, *The Polar Express* won the Caldecott Medal for children's literature in 1986. Publisher Houghton Mifflin says it has sold more than seven million copies.

The researcher on the other of the phone explained to Braid that the book was going to be made into a movie, and a ground-breaking one at that. Fully animated, it would be the first full-length film using "digital capture" to animate not only inanimate components such as the train but also its human characters. To that end, the producers wanted to present as realistic a vision of a steam locomotive as

▲ A sound engineer from Skywalker Sound aims his digital microphones at the cylinders of 1225's Standard MB stoker engine. Photo by Lawrence G. Sobczak.

◄ Snow covers the central Michigan countryside as 1225 roars down the track with a North Pole Express excursion. Photo by Jeff Mast.

▲ Skywalker sound engineers run their microphones the length of the engine to capture every sound. Photo by Lawrence G. Sobczak.

▶ The locomotive crew runs 1225 back and forth over the King Road grade crossing on the St. Charles Branch during the sound sessions for *The Polar Express*. Photo by Lawrence G. Sobczak.

possible, right down to every rivet and every hiss of steam. Was Braid interested?

Once he said "yes," things happened fast. Very quickly came a visit from Rick Carter, the movie's art director, who was traveling to Grand Rapids. Soon Braid began getting calls from the production staff, asking all kinds of questions about how a steam locomotive operates. These were followed quickly by other calls from another partner in the movie, Sony Pictures ImageWorks, an emerging force in the world of digital animation.

The designers received mechanical drawings of 1225 to load into their computers, but that wasn't enough. They wanted to know how a headlight would be replaced on 1225, so Braid sent a headlight bulb and a series of how-to photos. They wanted to know what coal looked like, so Braid sent some pieces of coal. They wanted to know how it sounded for a man to slide down the coal pile, so Braid's crew recorded one of crew doing it.

Big movies have long gestation periods, and it was quite awhile before two sound engineers from Lucas Digital Ltd.'s Skywalker Sound came to Owosso for a July 20, 2004, recording session. The Trust rolled out the red carpet for audio engineers Tim Nielson and Will Files and signed up its own 1225 operating crew of engineer Bill Wilson and firemen Rich Greter and Jeff Lis.

The session began with a fireup of the locomotive at 6 A.M., which was 3 A.M. for the sound crew, who had just flown in from California. Using a variety of microphones, a field audio mixer, and a 4-channel field hard-drive recorder, the Skywalker team committed to digital

audio tape every imaginable sound of 1225: whistle, bell, accelerating engine, engine coming to a stop, the butterfly doors of the firebox, coupling and uncoupling the engine, the air compressors, wheels slipping, dropping coal, a crewman sliding on the coal pile (again), shoveling coal.

Then the session moved to the St. Charles Branch, where the locomotive pulled a train of fourteen empty hopper cars to generate authentic sounds of 1225 at speed. The Shiawassee County Road Commission even closed one grade crossing to give the train nearly two miles of track to run without distractions. Several hours later, with sounds safely recorded, the train returned to Owosso, and the Skywalker team flew back to Hollywood.

The Polar Express opened in the fall of 2004, with Tom Hanks providing several of the voices, and the film digitally captured movements of several characters, including the train conductor, a ghostly hobo, and Santa Claus. The producers and the SRI even planned to run 1225 to Grand Rapids for the premiere, but CSX eventually backed out. The movie received mixed reviews from critics, whose reservations centered mostly on the strangeness of the human characters. Digital capture was still in its infancy.

But audiences were enchanted by 1225 and its train. From the moment the little boy wakes up from a deep sleep on Christmas Eve to witness the thundering arrival of the train on his quiet residential street, the viewer is overwhelmed by the majestic power of 1225. Indeed, the first half of the movie is a flat-out tribute to the locomotive, and although its high-speed stunts are flights of fancy, the machine itself is astonishingly realistic. Steam purists might grumble about the facelift on the smokebox, to match the book's artwork, but the rest of the movie engine is pure Lima.

The movie went on to gross $307 million worldwide, which was good for an animated film but not quite a blockbuster given the $165 million production costs. Still, *The Polar Express* has taken its place in the pantheon of Christmas movies, and millions of people have thrilled to the sights and sounds of 1225, if only via digital special effects.

Then there's the matter of Chris Van Allsburg's connection to 1225 and the implication of

the engine's "December 25" number. In interviews around the time of the premiere, Van Allsburg said he had encountered the engine in the 1960s on childhood visits to the MSU campus, and he was quoted as having been enchanted by its number. But in a subsequent November 2014 interview by Dean Pyers, the SRI's archivist, Van Allsburg indicated only a fleeting memory of a single encounter when his dad took him to an MSU football game. He said the number of the cab had made no particular impression.

▲ In a fanciful scene from *The Polar Express*, a leaning 1225 and its accurately detailed undercarriage shows the level of authenticity sought by the locomotive's animators. Photo licensed by Warner Bros. Entertainment Inc. All Rights Reserved.

REPRIEVE FOR A SISTER ENGINE

With all the attention 1225 began receiving after it became operational, it was easy to forget that one other Pere Marquette (PM) Berkshire had escaped the torch. The 1223 would never garner the fame of its living, breathing sister engine, but it is a surviving example of the Lima Super Power doctrine and therefore should not be overlooked.

Until some Michigan State University (MSU) students began turning wrenches on 1225, both PM 2-8-4s had plenty in common. Both were members of the N-1 class, delivered to the railroad by Lima within a couple of weeks of each other in late 1941. They are identical machines, so they presumably compiled nearly matching records of performance and availability for the decade they saw freight service. Both were in the group of retired engines stored at New Buffalo. And both were plucked out of the scrap line and sent back to Wyoming for a cosmetic restoration.

That's where the narratives diverge. While 1225 was the lucky recipient of a wealthy benefactor's largesse in 1957, 1223 spent another three years down in New Buffalo before it, too, was rescued as part of a fund-raising campaign aimed at schoolchildren in Detroit. The money they raised allowed for the donation of 1223 to the Michigan

State Fair, which displayed the locomotive behind the grandstand on the fairgrounds along Woodward Avenue in Detroit. For the next twenty years, the big Berkshire served as an inert diversion for fairgoers, its occasional maintenance left to the venerable Michigan Railroad Club.

Fast-forward to 1980. After two decades out in the elements, 1223 looked rough around the edges, having been the victim of the weather, reduced maintenance, and vandals. When State Fair management decided to enlarge the grandstand, 1223 had to go. There was a competition of sorts among a handful of municipalities and museums, and ultimately the state awarded the engine to the city of Grand Haven.

An attractive beach town just south of Muskegon, Grand Haven wasn't an obvious choice. The city had historically been served by the Grand Trunk Western (GTW) and the PM, but the PM line was a branch from Holland and far too light to support the use of the Berkshires. The closest 1223 ever got to Grand Haven was 22 miles to the southeast, on the PM main line. Nevertheless, Grand Haven wanted the engine, so on July 31, 1981, with the help of the National Guard, 1223 was carefully switched out of the fairgrounds and towed the 180 miles to Grand Haven via the GTW and CSX.

Today, 1223 is the star of a small but nicely maintained railroad exhibit on the site of Grand Haven's old GTW terminal. In addition to the 2-8-4, the display includes a PM auto-carrier boxcar and two cabooses, one PM and one GTW. The train is parked against the hulking backdrop of a concrete coaling tower. The 1223 is owned by Grand Haven's Tri-Cities Historical Museum, which partners with a local group of volunteers to keep the locomotive in sparkling condition.

Back in the 1970s, the Michigan Railroad Club declined to allow the MSU Railroad Club access to 1223's firebox grates, an unfortunate decision the students got around by using grates from a Chesapeake & Ohio engine in Ohio. Relations improved in Grand Haven, however, and the Steam Railroading Institute in Owosso has received some small but important parts off 1223, including grease cellars, which lubricate 1225's driving axles, and safety valves. These parts would have been exceedingly expensive to remanufacture. In return, the 1225 crew has occasionally helped out with public events run by the Tri-Cities Historical Museum. It's not a stretch to say that, seventy years after they were built, 1223 and 1225 remain close sisters.

Pere Marquette 1223 heads up a collection of vintage equipment at the former Grand Trunk Western site in Grand Haven. Photo by Jeff Mast.

CHAPTER 9

THE ONCE AND FUTURE BERKSHIRE

Lima never lost faith in its steam locomotives, even as the diesel was poking its nose into the roundhouse. In December 1940, the company produced an ad showing a locomotive engineer in classic overalls and a cap, kneeling in front of a small boy holding a model engine. Looming behind them, magnificently, is a Lima icon, one of Southern Pacific's streamlined 4-8-4 *Daylight* engines. "They'll still be using steam locomotives when you grow up, Sonny," the old man says, confidently.

It didn't turn out that way. In 1939, Electro-Motive built the first successful freight diesel. When 1225 was built in 1941, it was already obsolete. Even Lima's designers, the "scientists of steam," as David P. Morgan called them, couldn't stop what was coming. Within ten years of the ad, Lima would stop building steam locomotives after a gallant effort to keep them going with exotic ideas such as poppet valves and six-wheeling trailing trucks. Fittingly, the last Lima main-line steam engine was a Nickel Plate 2-8-4, No. 779, delivered in May 1949. By that time Lima had already merged with General Machinery Corporation to become Lima-Hamilton and enter the diesel market.

Few railroads enabled the diesel's total victory as quickly as the Pere Marquette (PM). When Lima began delivering 2-8-4s to the PM in 1937, the two parties would have rightfully expected

◄ The North Pole Express roars past the grain elevator at Carland in December 2013. Photo by Jeff Mast.

the new machines to last a quarter-century. Instead, when the railroad abolished steam in 1951, its last eleven PM Berkshires, the N-2 class of 1944, were virtually new.

Only one of those PM engines got the chance to live out its promise. Lima's engineers never would have dreamed that the unheralded 1225 would maximize its service miles by running deep into the twenty-first century. But run it did, across Michigan, across Ohio, down through Kentucky and West Virginia, and ultimately into the imaginations of millions of moviegoers.

◆   ◆   ◆

Although *The Polar Express* brought little direct revenue to 1225, the locomotive's appearance in the 2004 beloved Christmas movie came as the engine managed a sustained period of routine operations, if anything is routine with a seventy-year-old steam locomotive. The film led to the Steam Railroading Institute's (SRI's) lucrative North Pole Express trips. Launched as a series of short holiday excursions on the St. Charles Branch to the Saginaw County Fairgrounds in Chesaning, the trips ran to various destinations, sometimes using diesels from a cooperative Tuscola & Saginaw Bay (TSBY). The luckiest North Pole Express passengers got to ride behind 1225.

The goodwill around Owosso survived the 2006 transition of the TSBY into the Great Lakes Central (GLC), a new railroad owned by the holding company Federated Railways Inc. New GLC management has had the good sense to see the SRI as a paying customer, and 1225 has continued to flourish. In 2014, the Christmas trips alone attracted more than 8,000 passengers to a series of North Pole Express trips

► With the iconic Durand depot as a backdrop, 1225 leads a June 2008 special train for the shortline holding company RailAmerica. Photo by Jeff Mast.

to Ashley, 21 miles northwest of Owosso. Seasonal operations continued at Owosso, including the engineer- and fireman-for-an-hour program, rebranded, respectively, as "Your Hand on the Throttle" and "Your Hand on the Shovel."

Other opportunities have come 1225's way. In June 2008, the SRI was invited by the shortline company RailAmerica to use 1225 to pull an executive dinner train in the Saginaw–Bay City area on its Huron & Eastern, which operates 384 miles of track, mostly in the Thumb. On the ferry trip to Bay City, RailAmerica management surprised the steam crew by giving 1225 the opportunity to haul a twenty-car, 2,700-ton freight train, an assignment the Berkshire handled easily.

There were railfan trips, too. In October 2005, the SRI partnered with the Bluewater Chapter of the National Railway Historical Society to run a pair of excursions from Kawkawlin, near Bay City, to Gaylord over 100 miles of the former New York Central Mackinaw Division, now operated by Lake States Railway. It was the longest outing for

1225 since the West Virginia trek of 1991. The Saturday/Sunday trips each attracted more than 700 passengers and were so successful they were repeated in 2007.

With the flexibility that comes with a friendly railroad partner, 1225 also became popular in the boutique world of photo charters. The 1225 is a frequent prop for photographers and video producers who pay top dollar to shoot the engine hauling a vintage train of 1940s-era freight cars from the SRI collection. The carefully staged scenes often feature vintage automobiles and railroaders in period costume. A favorite location is the old Michigan Bean Company elevator in Henderson, on the St. Charles Branch. Spectacular but staged, these photos and videos have helped give 1225 a formidable Internet profile.

While the engine was running off all these productive miles, the SRI finally got a chance to build a facility worthy of its locomotive. In 2005, the organization won a federal grant, administered by the Michigan Department of Transportation, to pay a substantial part of the cost of building a massive circular concrete pit for the old New Buffalo turntable. Around the same time, the institute erected a two-track, 60-by-120-foot metal shop building to house 1225, replacing the old brick Ann Arbor edifice, which was razed.

◆   ◆   ◆

Performing regularly on the steam stage, 1225 also moved inexorably toward the deadline for another complete fifteen-year boiler inspection under Federal Railroad Administration (FRA) rules. The last reflueing had come in 1995, in time for the stillborn Scranton trip. Immediately thereafter, the rules governing boilers had changed.

In 2000, a blue-ribbon group of steam locomotive experts worked with FRA to revise the rules for the twenty-first century, replacing the traditional five-year requirement with one requiring an internal inspection every fifteen years or after 1,472 service days, whichever came first. The FRA had granted the SRI a waiver establishing August 5, 1995, as 1225's "start date," meaning the engine would have to be taken out of service in August 2010.

Two generations of workers had restored 1225 to be a living, breathing artifact, so there

◀ Pere Marquette 1225 races through the morning light with a photographers' special freight train in November 2014. Photo by Jeff Mast.

was never any question that the SRI would take a deep breath and try to raise the money to refurbish the boiler. But things had gotten more complicated. Not only would another boiler job be expensive, the institute itself had become a complex entity, with a staff to support, grounds to maintain, and lots of bills to pay. Laying up 1225 for a few months meant sidelining the main source of income for the SRI's $500,000 annual operating budget.

Big problems can hatch big ideas. The organization decided that a large-scale public event could attract enough visitors to raise significant money for 1225's boiler work, as well as bring revenue for other purposes. Inspired by a large gathering of steam locomotives on the Ohio Central Railroad in 2004, the 1225 team conceived of Train Festival 2009: a full weekend of steam operations, tours, and concessions to be based at the grounds in Owosso. The big draw would be a special guest locomotive, Nickel Plate 765, which had recently completed its own fifteen-year rebuild in Fort Wayne, Indiana.

It fell to the SRI's new executive director, T. J. Gaffney, to pull the festival together. It helped that the 1225 crew had nurtured strong ties with Ohio Central, a regional freight railroad whose 2004 festival was a big success. They also got an enthusiastic response from the Fort Wayne group. "We needed a big event to bring some money and notoriety to the SRI," recalls Gaffney. "Our whole idea was to put 1225 and 765 together again for the first time since Huntington. It would be a sort of reverse coming-out party for the Nickel Plate engine."[1]

Having the two Advisory Mechanical Committee (AMC) Berkshires perform together again would be spectacular enough, but Train

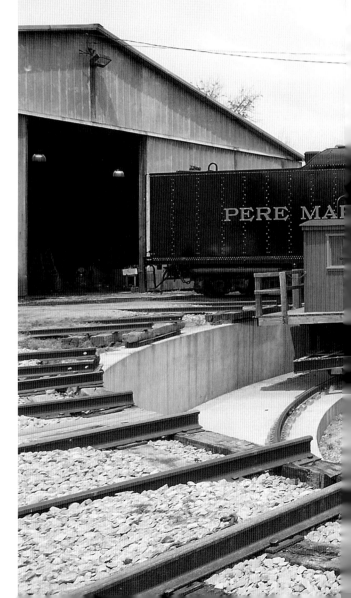

Pere Marquette 1225 rides the restored New Buffalo turntable at the Steam Railroading Institute in Owosso. Photo by Jeff Mast.

Iron horses gather at Train Festival 2009 (*from left*): Little River Railroad 0-4-0T No. 1, Little River 4-6-2 No. 110, Pere Marquette 1225, Southern Pacific 4-8-4 No. 4449, and Nickel Plate 2-8-4 No. 765. Photo by Mitch Goldman.

Festival 2009 picked up unexpected momentum in November 2008, this time in the form of a commitment from what is perhaps Lima's most famous locomotive. At a railroad preservation meeting in Milwaukee, Gaffney had a conversation with Doyle McCormack, whose group in Portland, Oregon, operates Southern Pacific (SP) 4-8-4 No. 4449, one of the orange-and-red streamlined speedsters famous for SP's Los Angeles–San Francisco *Daylight* trains.

McCormack had heard about Owosso's Train Festival. "How'd you like to have the girl there?" he asked Gaffney. It was a sensational idea. To have all three of these great Lima locomotives together, in steam, would be unprecedented. But there was a missing piece: even with approval from several Class I railroads along the route and the backing of Amtrak as a sponsor, 4449 could never make the 4,000-mile trip to Owosso and back without having a way to pay for it.

"I was stumbling for words," Gaffney says, "but then who walks in on our conversation but Steve Sandberg. He was the missing piece." Steve Sandberg had established himself as a successful main-line steam operator with Milwaukee Road 4-8-4 No. 261, the Minneapolis-based engine that starred at Steamtown in Scranton in 1995. Although his locomotive was out of service for the time being, Sandberg's fleet of passenger cars was available. A couple of months' worth of telephone conversations led to a novel arrangement. By leasing Sandberg's cars, 4449 could haul revenue passengers one-way across the western United States and back, perhaps generating enough revenue to bring the *Daylight* engine to Owosso.

The scheme worked. On July 2, 2009, 4449 headed out on its long eastward journey, hauling passengers out of various departure points in Montana, North Dakota, Minnesota, Wisconsin, and Michigan. The 4-8-4 arrived in Owosso on July 20 amid considerable fanfare.

The festival was a mixed bag for the SRI. Huge crowds showed up over the three days to thrill to the sights and sounds of a steam show no one could have ever predicted. It was amazing enough to have two Lima Berkshires together in steam. It was quite another thing to have the ultimate California engine doing the same thing. Gaffney called it "Limapalooza."

There were also a number of other smaller, live engines at the event, including Little River

Railroad 4-6-2 No. 110, which operated in tourist service between Quincy and Coldwater, Michigan; and 4-4-0 No. 63, the Chicago-based *Leviathan*, a completely new locomotive built as a replica of an 1860s-era engine, complete with balloon stack and gold leaf lettering.

The SRI estimated the final attendance figure for Train Festival at approximately 32,000 people, a spectacular turnout for a town with a population of 15,000. The festival was a boon for hotels, restaurants, and other businesses.

◆　　◆　　◆

One thing Train Festival 2009 didn't do was raise substantial money for 1225. In fact, it wasn't a good weekend at all for the host locomotive. Early in the morning on Friday, 1225 blew a flue in the rear flue sheet, shooting steam into the firebox and the cab. The crew on night watch quickly dumped the fire and got the injector shooting more water into the boiler. In fact, two tubes ended up failing, demonstrating that the set of flues from 1995 had reached the end of their fifteen-year service life. With that, 1225 was set aside for the rest of the festival, the spotlight shifting to 765 and 4449.

Looking back, Gaffney views Train Festival 2009 as a success for the SRI, if not necessarily 1225. "It allowed us to go from being a glorified junkyard to a site that a lot of people can be proud of. That event helped us finish the grounds, we put in a miniature live-steam railroad, we improved the interior of the museum and our water and electrical service. This transitioned us from being a club into being a real living museum."

Owosso's Train Festival also demonstrated once again the resourcefulness and resilience of 1225's caretakers. In the years following the festival, the SRI continued to raise money toward the fifteen-year rebuild of the locomotive. Through a combination of grants, donations, loans, and museum revenue, the organization managed to plow another $850,000-plus into the engine.

This time, in addition to replacing the flues and tubes, the SRI crew and contractors rebuilt the entire firebox, including installing another set of new thermic syphons. When 1225 emerged from its own shop in October

▲ Engineer Greg Udolf (*right*) and fireman Rob Gruich put the 1225 through its paces. Photo by Jeff Mast.

◀ Van Sweringen "cousins": Pere Marquette 1225 and NKP 765 team up on August 30, 2009, in a private charter for Lerro Productions. Photo by Mitch Goldman.

2013, its boiler was arguably in better shape than at any point since Lima pushed it out of the factory on that gray day in November 1941.

◆　　◆　　◆

The landscape that 1225 inhabited all those years before Owosso is largely gone. The engine crews that ran the Berkshires wouldn't recognize their old territory. Although CSX's former PM main line is still a first-class piece of railroad, it runs far fewer trains than in the old days. In fact, for a few years beginning in the 1990s, CSX put up most of its Michigan lines for sale, hoping to find a regional railroad to take over. Nothing came of it.

Wyoming is emblematic of the changes. Although CSX's freight yard remains busy, 1225's onetime home terminal is nearly gone. The roundhouse and the concrete coaling tower were razed years ago. So was the power plant, where Ken Pelton kept the boiler running into the 1970s. The monstrous erecting hall still stands off by itself, but it serves no railroad purpose; a local firm uses it as an industrial warehouse.

Nor is there much to see in Lima, Ohio, 1225's birthplace. The city of Lima does have Nickel Plate 779 on display in a local park, and the Allen County Historical Society is an excellent repository of Lima Locomotive Works archives. But the site of the old plant on South Main Street is a vast empty lot, marked by weeds and rubble and surrounded by a rusty chain-link fence.

There is even less to see at 1225's old home on the Michigan State University (MSU) campus. The section of Stadium Road that ran past the engine was removed, and the original Project 1225 site has been carefully landscaped with grass and new sidewalks, bordered by the Spartans' dramatic football practice facility. The university has erased

The Steam Railroading Institute's prized artifact receives maintenance inside the new engine shed at Owosso in June 2009. Photo by Jeff Mast.

all evidence of what happened here when a band of single-minded students tried to do the impossible, goading themselves with the slogan "It'll never run."

But it did run. Someone came along to finish the impossible. The engine has found a new home at the SRI, where it is safe from the elements, safe from the scrappers, safe from Jack Breslin. Since 1988, 1225 has run over thousands of miles of railroad. It promises to run thousands more, ready to demonstrate once again the power and majesty of Lima Super Power, a birthright that traces all the way back to Will Woodard's A-1 of 1925.

Author Chris Van Allsburg may barely remember the steam locomotive he crawled over as a kid on the MSU campus, but his most memorable advice from *The Polar Express*, voiced magically in the movie by Tom Hanks, applies to everyone who has played a role in the life of 1225: "One thing about trains. It doesn't matter where they're going. What matters is deciding to get on."

THE PERIPATETIC RAILWAY POST OFFICE

When the Michigan State University (MSU) Railroad Club acquired a Railway Post Office (RPO) from the Grand Trunk Western (GTW) in 1972, preservation of a significant historical artifact was far from members' minds. The club members simply wanted a safe place to store tools and perform minor mechanical work, in close proximity to 1225. But the car they bought that summer for $500, GTW 9683, represented an iconic piece of American railroad history.

The post office began using trains as early as 1832, when the postmaster general tapped New Jersey's Camden & Amboy Railroad for a mail route. Rapid expansion led to the creation in 1869 of the Railway Mail Service. By the time car 9683 was delivered new to the GTW in 1914, thousands of mail clerks were working aboard hundreds of RPO cars, sorting mail every night as the nation's passenger trains sped from city to city.

The atmosphere aboard cars such as 9683 was pure urgency. The train picked up mail at virtually every city and hamlet along the route, sometimes at full speed by use of a long mail hook, which a clerk extended to "catch" canvas mail pouches hanging at trackside. Inside the cars, nearly every square inch was crammed with bag racks, drawers, boxes, and cubbyholes marked for various postal addresses along the route. The clerks—all of which were U.S. Post Office employees—would sort thousands of letters and packages en route for delivery either to intermediate stations or to major post offices adjacent to big-city terminals.

When the railroad club members took delivery of 9683, they found a nearly pristine RPO interior, filled with most of the necessary mail equipment, including the big hook. Painted a utilitarian green, the interior offered plenty of places to store tools, lubricants, work clothes, and small locomotive parts. The cubbyholes still carried the names of various towns along the GTW system, big and small: Edwardsburg, Battle Creek, Millett, Swartz Creek, Imlay City, Port Huron, along with the names of cities and towns in California for cross-platform delivery to Santa Fe trains at Chicago's Dearborn Station.

The 9683 made the initial transition to Owosso when 1225 was moved there from East Lansing in 1983. But with an entire locomotive shop at their disposal, members of the new Michigan State Trust for Railway Preservation relied less and less on the RPO. Facing major repairs to the roof and car body, the Trust sold the car around 1988 to another group in Cleveland, the Midwest Railway Historical Society, which only coveted the car's 5-by-9-inch roller bearings. The new group scrapped the car.

But not before providing for another chapter for 9683. The interior furnishings were sold to the U.S. Postal Museum, an associate of the Smithsonian Institution, for installation of a new exhibit at the museum's home in the former Washington, D.C., post office adjacent to Union Station. About half the interior was restored and placed inside a replica car body of a Southern Railway RPO. Alas, the cubbyholes were relabeled with generic U.S. place names. But the overall impression is authentic.

A close cousin of 9683 also survives. Around the same time that MSU students were shopping for their RPO on the GTW scrap line in Battle Creek back in 1971, a contingent from the Illinois Railway Museum (IRM) was doing the same thing. Today, RPO 9695, also a 1914 produced of the Pressed Steel Car Company, resides in the IRM collection at Union, northwest of Chicago.

▶ Meticulously restored, the interior of Project 1225's RPO survives today inside a replica car body at the National Postal Museum in Washington, D.C. Courtesy of Smithsonian's National Postal Museum.

Steam Locomotive Classification Systems

VARIOUS SYSTEMS FOR THE CLASSIFICATION of steam locomotives have been proposed and are used to a greater or less extent. All are based on wheel or axle arrangements.

Whyte's System. The system commonly used in this country and in Great Britain is the one proposed by F. M. Whyte. In this system numerals are used to represent the number of wheels in each group starting at the front end, the first denoting the number of wheels in the leading truck, the second the number of drivers and the third the number of wheels in the trailing truck. In articulated locomotives a numeral is used for each group of drivers. The numerals are usually separated by hyphens. The diagrams and tables below show the application of this system to most types of locomotives now in use.

American Locomotive Company's System. This is the same as the Whyte system but hyphens are omitted. Following the classification figures the letter C may be added to denote compound, S to denote superheated and T to denote tank instead of separate tender. In addition a second set of figures is then added to denote the weight in nearest 1,000 lb. Examples—282 S 241 denoting a super-heated Mikado weighing 241,000 lb. and 2882 CS 563 a compound superheated articulated locomotive weighing 563,000 lb.

Lima Locomotive Works, Inc., uses the same system but includes hyphens. Example, 282-S-241.

Baldwin Locomotive Works' System. The classification system which was developed by this company and used until recently was outlined in the 1941 edition of the Locomotive Cyclopedia. The Baldwin Locomotive Works are now using the Whyte system.

French System. This is similar to the Whyte system but the numerals denote axles instead of wheels. In this system a Pacific type would be classified as a 2-3-1 instead of a 4-6-2.

German or Continental System. In this system capital letters A. B. C. D. etc. are used to denote the number of pairs of coupled wheels or driving axles,—1, 2, 3, 4 etc.—while numerals are used to denote the number of axles in the trucks. In the German system a Pacific type locomotive would be classified as a 2-C-1. In this system, should there be no leading or no trailing truck, the numeral 0 is not employed as in the Whyte system. As examples, an Eight-Wheel Switcher is a Type D and a Ten-Wheel Locomotive a Type 2-C.

Locomotives with 2-Wheel Leading Trucks

2-4-0	4-Coupled
2-4-2	Columbia
2-6-0	Mogul
2-6-2	Prairie
2-8-0	Consolidation
2-8-2	Mikado
2-8-4	Berkshire
2-10-0	Decapod
2-10-2	Santa Fe
2-10-4	Texas

Locomotives with 4-Wheel Leading Trucks

4-4-0	American—8-Wheel
4-4-2	Atlantic
4-6-0	10-Wheel
4-6-2	Pacific
4-6-4	Hudson
4-8-0	12-Wheel
4-8-2	Mountain
4-8-4	Northern
4-10-0	Mastodon
4-10-2	So. Pacific
4-12-2	Union Pacific

Switching Locomotives

0-4-0	4-Wheel Switcher
0-6-0	6-Wheel Switcher
0-8-0	8-Wheel Switcher
0-10-0	10-Wheel Switcher

Articulated Locomotives (Partial)

0-6-6-0	
2-6-6-2	
0-8-8-0	
2-8-8-0	
2-8-8-2	

Note: Articulated Locomotives recently built have been of the following types: 2-6-6-2, 2-6-6-4, 2-6-6-6, 4-6-6-4, 2-8-8-2, 2-8-8-4, 4-8-8-2 and 4-8-8-4.

Tank Locomotives (Partial)

0-4-0 T	
0-4-2 T	
0-4-4 T	Forney 4-Coupled
2-4-2 T	
2-4-4 T	
0-6-0 T	
0-6-2 T	
0-6-4 T	Forney 6-Coupled
4-6-4 T	Baltic
0-8-0 T	

► During the steam era, the *Locomotive Cyclopedia* was widely regarded by railroad master mechanics as the "bible" of their profession. It was a fixture in the offices of roundhouses and repair shops across North America. The *Cyclopedia* always included this explanation and chart for the Whyte Classification System, which was the generally accepted method for classifying steam locomotives by wheel arrangement and common name. Frederick Methvan Whyte, a mechanical engineer for the New York Central, devised the system around 1900.

From the *Locomotive Cyclopedia of American Practice . . . Fourteenth Edition* (New York: Simmons-Boardman Publishing Corporation, 1950–52), 499.

ACKNOWLEDGMENTS

Like Project 1225, this book is possible only because so many people were willing to pitch in. I'm deeply grateful for their assistance. But before I give them their due, I must provide full disclosure: although I wrote the narrative from the standard perspective of the third-person narrator, the truth is, I lived much of this story.

When I arrived at Michigan State University (MSU) as a sophomore in September 1970 (a transfer from Albion College), I knew nothing of 1225. I was a *Trains* magazine reader and railroad enthusiast, but Pere Marquette steam locomotives were mostly unknown to me. Early that fall, though, I was walking east from Holden Hall and, much to my surprise, encountered 1225, a massive presence on my route to class. More important, a couple of guys were doing something on the engine. One of them was Randy Paquette.

What I learned from Randy that day galvanized me.

"We're going to restore the engine and run it!" Absurd as that notion was, I was utterly taken in, partly by Randy's infectious passion and partly because, as anyone could see, 1225 is a magnificent machine. Somehow, seeing this exquisite product of the Lima Locomotive Works in full flight was an irresistible prospect. I joined the MSU Railroad Club almost on the spot. I spent the better part of the next three years throwing myself into Project 1225. I even managed to serve as president of the club 1972–73. The experience was brutal on my GPA and provoked scorn from my parents, but my involvement in the locomotive quite literally led me to an unlikely and satisfying career.

I'm a very lucky author. It's not often that you get a chance to write your first book on the direct invitation of your publisher. But that's just what happened when my editor and mentor in all this, Gabe Dotto, contacted me.

When I explained my personal connection to 1225 and how much of it could be told in the first person, we agreed this could be problematic. I couldn't see how the storyteller could switch perspectives without disrupting the narrative. Finally, Gabe suggested I just leave myself out of the story and own up to it in the Acknowledgments. I'm grateful for that advice, and hope that you, my reader, will decide this approach worked. Thank you, Gabe, for your wisdom and endless patience with a first-time book author.

A word about Randy Paquette. I'm in the camp that says 1225 would never have come to life without him. Randy was the prime mover of the MSU Railroad Club, and his almost single-minded devotion drove the early progress on the restoration. Although life circumstances obliged Randy to step back from 1225 after the 1975 fire-up, his hard work and influence are in evidence every time our 2-8-4 turns a wheel. Had he merely walked past the engine on his way to class one day in 1969, I believe 1225 would have faced an unhappy fate, either as scrap metal or as another rusting hulk at an overburdened railroad museum. Randy and his wife, Betty, offered me wonderful hospitality in the research phase of the book. A few months later Randy made key suggestions for the manuscript, for which I'm very grateful.

Here's a similar nod to another MSU comrade in arms, Aarne Frobom, who offered unsparing editing of my text.

I met Aarne at MSU in 1971. His long tenure with 1225, from the early MSU Railroad Club days right through to his leadership at the Steam Railroading Institute, makes him an essential source. Aarne writes brilliantly about the history of technology, and someday he should write his own book about 1225. It will be better than mine.

Several other people offered critical contributions. My old friend from the club Chuck Julian sent me copious notes about Project 1225 in the MSU days. Chuck had a deeper mastery of mechanical engineering than anyone in the club. I don't know what we would have done without him. When the project fell into troubling limbo after 1975, it was Chuck who stepped up and changed the course of his life to save the engine.

Thanks, also, to David Jones, longtime 1225 historian and author of his own delightful account of Project 1225, "The Spartan Locomotive," from the April 1989 issue of *Trains*. David became a scholar of Pere Marquette steam, and his various writings on 1225 were invaluable. The same could be said for T. J. Gaffney and Dean Pyers, who helped me understand key aspects of the locomotive's Owosso tenure. Their book, *Pere Marquette 1225*, a 2014 release from Arcadia Publishing, is a flavorful, picture-driven review of the 1225 story. It was a great resource for me, and I'm pleased and flattered that T.J. and Dean have seen our two books as complementary.

Images really drive a story like this, and I'm indebted to a number of photographers. Chief among them is my dear friend John B. Corns, an acclaimed lensman who for many years had a distinguished career as CSX Transportation's chief photographer. John showed up at the 1225 enclosure in April 1971 after reading about the project in Mike Eagleson's "In Search of Steam" column in the old *Railroad* magazine. We became fast friends. He set up shop as Project 1225's chief chronicler, giving the club an amazing visual record of those early years. Over the decades, John and I became partners on numerous journalism projects for *Trains* magazine. Thanks, Mr. Eagleson, for introducing two lifelong friends.

I'm indebted to a number of other key photographers. Jeff Mast was a stalwart, providing beautiful photographs of 1225 in the Owosso era. Similarly generous was Michael Valentine, a gifted shooter who has followed the engine for years. Together with Mitch Goldman, they stepped up when MSU Press approved the book's color section. Jay Williams, an Indianapolis friend from the MSU days, shot the October 1975 fire-up and key moments a few years later in Owosso. Victor Hand, whose magisterial photos have graced the pages of *Trains* for more than forty years, provided essential photos of two high points in 1225's excursion career: the October 1990 CSX freight to Grand Rapids, and the August 1991 trip to Huntington,

West Virginia. I also want to thank Larry Sobczak for allowing me to use his photos of the Skywalker Sound team recording 1225 for *The Polar Express*, as well as Jim O'Donnell for arranging an interior photo of the Railway Post Office (RPO) car at the National Postal Museum. And it's not all about the photos. I was able to recruit our gifted mapmaker from *Trains*, Bill Metzger, for the beautiful Pere Marquette system map. Bill approaches cartography as a storyteller, and the extra touches on this map—roundhouses and coaling towers, for instance—are all his idea.

In addition to individual photographers, I'm grateful to staff members from several historic archives. Foremost was the indulgence of my employer, Kalmbach Publishing Co., which allowed me to plumb various files in its David P. Morgan Memorial Library. These images arrived at *Trains* in the 1940s and 1950s from a host of intrepid steam-era photographers hoping to get their credit lines in the magazine. Given the time I spent raiding the files, I'm especially grateful for the patience of librarian Tom Hoffmann.

There were other key collections. Portia Vescio helped me track down several important photos from the MSU Archives. Charles Bates, of the Allen County Historical Society, provided critical images from the society's splendid Lima Locomotive Works files, notably a portrait of Will Woodard. Tom Dixon and Brandy Dudley offered several pictures from the Chesapeake & Ohio Historical Society's excellent online archives; in its heyday, the Chesapeake & Ohio hired some of the best industrial photographers in America, evident in the William Rittase photos of the turntable and wartime maintenance at Wyoming.

In addition to the editing and fact-checking provided by Randy Paquette and Aarne Frobom, I'm grateful for the services of Rob McGonigal, my colleague at Kalmbach and longtime editor of our *Classic Trains* magazine. Rob is a meticulous, deeply knowledgeable editor, and he caught a number of errors that would have left me embarrassed. I like to think we've been doing that for each other all these years. I'm grateful to another colleague, Kathi Kube of *Discover* magazine, for loaning me "The Steam Locomotive in America," Alfred W. Bruce's indispensable midcentury reference. Thanks also to another longtime friend and coworker, my former boss J. David Ingles, senior editor of *Classic Trains*, for his brilliant editing of the map. For the foreword, my deep appreciation goes to Bill Withuhn, who so beautifully places 1225 in a large context. In July 1987 Bill and I shared a different steam locomotive cab— Pennsylvania Railroad K4s 1361—and I learned firsthand how effective a scholar of engineering history can be with a locomotive throttle in his left hand.

Finally, and most importantly, thanks to my wife, Alison, for her steadfast support of my railroad passion over the past forty-plus years. Some of my friends often tell me she's the best thing that ever happened to me, and they're right. She shares in the story, too. As an advertising major at MSU in the early 1970s, she could write a dandy slogan for a steam locomotive.

Despite the best efforts of my editors, readers, and sources, errors in fact or judgment are bound to creep into the narrative. For all of them, I'm completely responsible.

Notes and Bibliography

CHAPTER 1 _____

Notes

1. White, *American Locomotives*, xxi.

2. Bruce, *Steam Locomotive in America*, 25.

3. Cook, *Super-Power*, 11–12.

Published Works

Bruce, Alfred W. *The Steam Locomotive in America*. New York: W. W. Norton, 1952.

Cook, Richard J. *Super Power Steam Locomotives*. San Marino, Calif.: Golden West Books, 1966.

Drury, George H. *Guide to North American Steam Locomotives*. Waukesha, Wis.: Kalmbach Books, 1993.

Gaffney, T. J., and Dean Pyers. *Pere Marquette 1225*. Charleston, S.C.: Arcadia Publishing, 2014.

Hirsimaki, Eric. *Lima: The History*. Mulkilteo, Wash.: Hundman Publishing, 1986.

Lamb, J. Parker. *Perfecting the American Steam Locomotive*. Bloomington: Indiana University Press, 2003.

Middleton, William D., George M. Smerk, and Roberta L. Diehl. *Encyclopedia of North American Railroads*. Bloomington: Indiana University Press, 2007.

White, John H., Jr. *American Locomotives: An Engineering History, 1830–1880*. 1968. Reprint, Baltimore: Johns Hopkins University Press, 1997.

CHAPTER 2 _____

Notes

1. Haberman, *Van Sweringens*, 74.

2. Rehor, *Nickel Plate Story*, 236.

3. Rehor and Horning, *Berkshire Era*, 9.

Published Works

Cook, Richard J. *Super Power Steam Locomotives*. San Marino, Calif.: Golden West Books, 1966.

Drury, George H. *Guide to North American Steam Locomotives*. Waukesha, Wis.: Kalmbach Books, 1993.

Gaffney, T. J., and Dean Pyers. *Pere Marquette 1225*. Charleston, S.C.: Arcadia Publishing, 2014.

Haberman, Ian S. *The Van Sweringens of Cleveland: The Biography of an Empire*. Cleveland: Western Reserve Historical Society, 1979.

Huddleston, Eugene, Philip Shuster, and Alvin Staufer. *C&O Power*. Medina, Ohio: Alvin F. Staufer, 1965.

Lamb, J. Parker. *Perfecting the American Steam Locomotive*. Bloomington: Indiana University Press, 2003.

Middleton, William D., George Smerk, and Roberta L. Diehl. *Encyclopedia of North American Railroads*. Bloomington: Indiana University Press, 2007.

Million, Art, and Thomas W. Dixon Jr. *Pere Marquette Power*. Alderson, W.Va.: Chesapeake & Ohio Historical Society, 1984.

Morgan, David P. "It's Dungarees for the Diesel." *Trains* (May 1953).

Rehor, John A. *The Nickel Plate Story*. Milwaukee: Kalmbach Books, 1965.

Rehor, John A., and Philip T. Horning. *The Berkshire Era: A Pictorial Review of the Nickel Plate Road, 1934–1958*. Rocky River, Ohio: John A. Rehor, 1967.

CHAPTER 3

Notes

1. Morgan, "World War II," *Trains* (November 1965), 27.
2. Million and Dixon, *Pere Marquette Power*, 137.
3. *Railway Age*, April 5, 1947, 705.

Published Works

Haberman, Ian S. *The Van Sweringens of Cleveland: The Biography of an Empire*. Cleveland: Western Reserve Historical Society, 1979.

Heimburger, Donald J., and John Kelly. *Trains to Victory: America's Railroads in World War II*. Forest Park, Ill.: Heimburger House, 2009.

Hill, David A. "Inspection of Pere Marquette Railway, January 9–13, 1945." *Trains* magazine collection.

Huddleston, Eugene, Philip Shuster, and Alvin Staufer. *C&O Power*. Medina, Ohio: Alvin F. Staufer, 1965.

Middleton, William D., George Smerk, and Roberta L. Diehl. *Encyclopedia of North American Railroads*. Bloomington: Indiana University Press, 2007.

Million, Art, and Thomas W. Dixon Jr. *Pere Marquette Power*. Alderson, W.Va.: Chesapeake & Ohio Historical Society, 1984.

Morgan, David P. "World War II: The Greatest Test of All." *Trains* (November 1965).

Our GM Scrapbook. Milwaukee: Kalmbach Books, 1971.

CHAPTER 4

Notes

1. Jones, "Spartan Locomotive," *Trains* (April 1989), 44.

2. Paquette interview, November 2014.

3. Jones, "Spartan Locomotive."

Interviews by Author

Paquette, Randy. November 2014.

Published Works

Conrad, J. David. *The Steam Locomotive Directory of North America*. Vol. 1, *Eastern United States and Canada*. Polo, Ill.: Transportation Trails, 1988.

Jones, David. "The Spartan Locomotive." *Trains* (April 1989).

Keefe, Kevin P. "An Unlikely Acquisition." *Project 1225* (October–November 1973).

"Locomotive Received as Museum Exhibit." *Michigan State News*, June 12, 1957.

Middleton, William D., George M. Smerk, and Roberta L. Diehl. *Encyclopedia of North American Railroads*. Bloomington: Indiana University Press, 2007.

Million, Art, and Thomas W. Dixon Jr. *Pere Marquette Power*. Alderson, W.Va.: Chesapeake & Ohio Historical Society, 1984.

Thomas, David A. *Michigan State College, John Hannah and the Creation of a World University, 1926–1969*. East Lansing: Michigan State University Press, 2008.

CHAPTER 5

Notes

1. Paquette interview, November 2014.

2. Julian interview, March 2015.

3. Paquette interview, November 2014.

4. Paquette interview, November 2014.

5. Julian interview, March 2015.

6. *Encomium*, November 2009.

7. Julian interview, March 2015.

Interviews by Author

Julian, Chuck. March 2015.

Paquette, Randy. November 2014.

Published Works

Baker, Rollin H. (quoted). *Project 1225* (October–November 1973).

Edmonson, Harold A. *Journey to Amtrak: The Year History Rode the Passenger Train*. Milwaukee: Kalmbach Publishing, 1972.

Encomium: Rollin Harold Baker. Mammalogy Papers, University of Nebraska Museum. University of Nebraska–Lincoln, October 2009.

Gaffney, T. J., and Dean Pyers. *Pere Marquette 1225*. Charleston, S.C.: Arcadia Publishing, 2014.

Jones, David. "The Spartan Locomotive." *Trains* (April 1989).

Weinman, Michael R. "All That Glitters Is Not Stainless Steel." *Trains* (January 1975).

CHAPTER 6

Notes

1. Julian interview, March 2015.

2. Frobom interview, March 2015.

3. Scovill, taped conversation, October 2009.

4. Julian interview, March 2015.

Interviews by Author

Frobom, Aarne. November 2014.

Julian, Chuck. March 2015.

Paquette, Randy. November 2014.

Other Unpublished Sources

Campbell, Mark G. Conversation aboard 1225 excursion, recorded by Randy Paquette, October 3, 2009.

Julian, Chuck. Conversation aboard 1225 excursion, recorded by Randy Paquette, October 3, 2009.

Scovill, Roger. Conversation aboard 1225 excursion, recorded by Randy Paquette, October 3, 2009.

Published Works

Drury, George H. *The Historical Guide to North American Railroads*. Milwaukee: Kalmbach Books, 1985.

Gaffney, T. J., and Dean Pyers. *Pere Marquette 1225*. Charleston, S.C.: Arcadia Publishing, 2014.

Grace Under Pressure. Kansas City: International Brotherhood of Boilermakers, Iron Ship Builders, Blacksmiths, Forgers & Helpers, AFL-CIO, 2006.

Jones, David. "The Spartan Locomotive." *Trains* (April 1989).

CHAPTER 7

Notes

1. Crawford, "June Fire-Up Is a Mixed Bag," *Project 1225* (Summer 1987), 3.

2. Frobom interview, March 2015.

3. Keefe, "It'll Never Run," *Trains* (November 1991), 6.

4. Keefe, "It'll Never Run," *Trains* (November 1991), 8.

5. Keefe, "It'll Never Run," *Trains* (November 1991), 8.

6. Warrick, *Ann Arbor Railroad in Color*, 3.

Interviews by Author

Frobom, Aarne. January 2015.

Published Works

Crawford, Rodney. "June Fire-Up Is a Mixed Bag." *Project 1225* (Summer 1987).

Gaffney, T. J., and Dean Pyers. *Pere Marquette 1225*. Charleston, S.C.: Arcadia Publishing, 2014.

Jones, David. "The Spartan Locomotive." *Trains* (April 1989).

Keefe, Kevin P. "A Hurricane of Steam." *Trains* (November 1991).

———. "'It'll Never Run'—But It Did." *Trains* (November 1991).

———. "With Apologies to Fred and Ginger." *Trains* (November 1987).

The 1225 Goes Home. Project 1225 (December 1990).

Warrick, Robert I. *Ann Arbor Railroad in Color: History & Operations, 1869–1976.* Scotch Plains, N.J.: Morning Sun Books, 2008.

CHAPTER 8

Notes

1. Frobom interview, March 2015.
2. Frobom interview, March 2015.

Interviews by Author

Frobom, Aarne. January 2015.

Interviews by Others

Van Allsburg, Chris. Interviewed by Dean Pyers, November 2014.

Published Works

Frobom, Aarne. "What Was the Thermic Syphon?" *Project 1225* (April 1992).

Keefe, Kevin P. "They Came to Steamtown." *Trains* (October 1995).

Lustig, David. "Hollywood's Steam Locomotive." *Trains* (January 2005).

CHAPTER 9

Note

1. Gaffney interview, January 2015.

Interviews by Author

Frobom, Aarne. October 2014.

Gaffney, T. J. January 2015.

Knudsen, Gary. October 2014.

Published Works

Frobom, Aarne. "The 15-Year Boiler Inspection." *Member's Bulletin*, Michigan State Trust for Railway Preservation, December 2007.

Gaffney, T. J., and Dean Pyers. *Pere Marquette 1225.* Charleston, S.C.: Arcadia Publishing, 2014.

Hadder, Eric. "Critical Checkup for Steam." *Trains* (May 2013).

Johnson, Jason. "Train Festival 2009." *Project 1225* (Spring 2010).

Lima Locomotive Works ad. *Railway Age* (December 1940).

Pere Marquette #1225 Hauls Revenue Freight for Rail America. Member's Bulletin, Michigan State Trust for Railway Preservation, August 2008.

Withuhn, William L. "Steam, Steel and Safety." *Trains* (May 2000).

INDEX

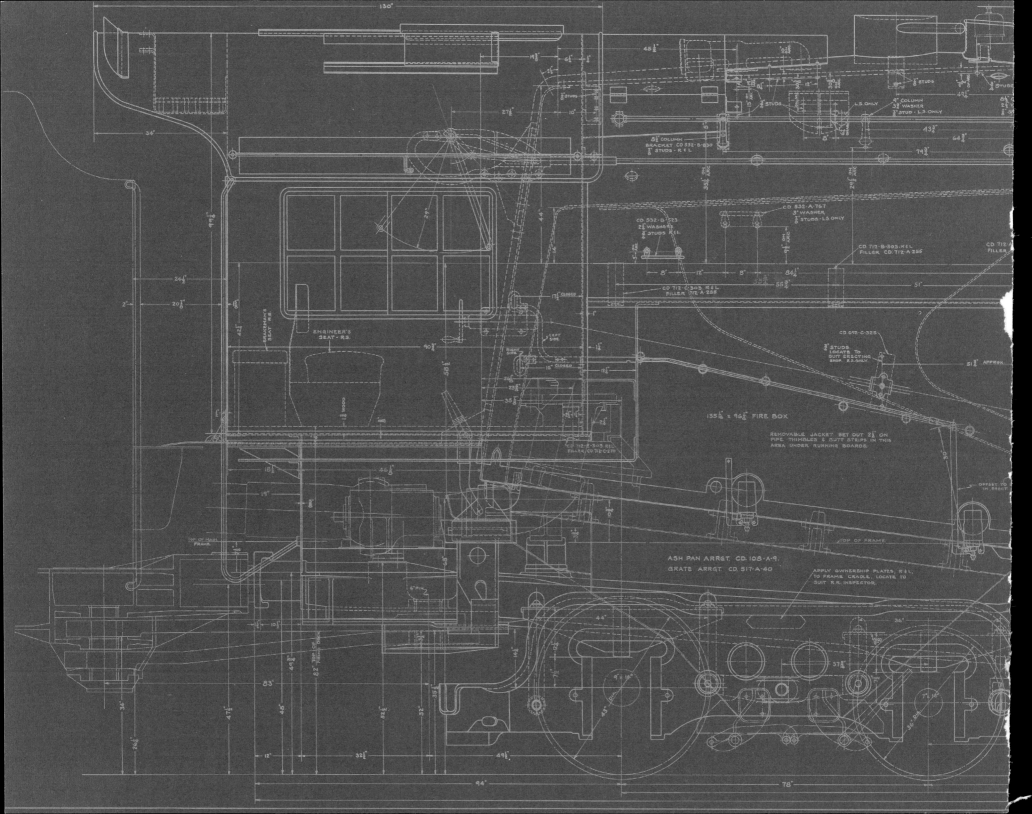